Contents

70047181

429.09
BRI

Test Your Professional English

Law

Nick Brieger

Series Editor: Nick Brieger

PENGUIN ENGLISH

COLEG GLAN HAFREN LRC PARADE

Pearson Education Limited
Edinburgh Gate
Harlow
Essex CM20 2JE, England
and Associated Companies throughout the world.

ISBN-13: 978-0-582-46898-6
ISBN-10: 0-582-46898-1

First published 2002
Text copyright © Nick Brieger 2002

Fifth impression 2006

Designed and typeset by Pantek Arts Ltd, Maidstone, Kent
Test Your format devised by Peter Watcyn-Jones
Illustrations by Mike Flannagan
Printed in China
SWTC/05

All rights reserved; no part of this publication may be reproduced, stored in a retrieval system, or transmitted in any form or by any means, electronic, mechanical, photocopying, recording or otherwise, without the prior written permission of the Publishers.

Acknowledgements
Thanks to the many students at York Associates who contributed to and trialled these materials; also to Jane Durkin at Penguin for her support with all the TYPE titles.

Published by Pearson Education Limited in association with Penguin Books Ltd, both companies being subsidiaries of Pearson plc.

For a complete list of the titles available in the Penguin Readers series please write to your local Pearson Education office or to contact:
Penguin English Marketing Department, Pearson Education,
Edinburgh Gate, Harlow, Essex, CM20 2JE.

To the student

Do you use English in your work? Or is it a part of your studies? Maybe you are a legal professional; or a student of law. Whatever your background, if you need to improve your legal English, the tests in this book will help. They will check your knowledge of basic legal concepts, key words and essential expressions so that you can communicate more effectively and confidently in your work and for your studies.

There are eight sections in the book. The first section in this book is an introduction to general legal terms and concepts. The remaining seven sections each cover a different area of law – from contracts and agreements to international law. You can either work through the book from beginning to end or select chapters according to your interests and needs.

Many tests also have tips (advice) on language, language learning and professional information. Do read these explanations and tips: they are there to help you.

To make the book more challenging and more fun, many different kinds of tests are used, including sentence transformation, gap-filling, word families, multiple choice and crosswords. There is a key at the back of the book so that you can check your answers; and a word list to help you revise key vocabulary.

Your vocabulary is an essential resource for effective communication. Remember that the more words you know, the more meanings you can express. This book will help you develop your specialist vocabulary still further. Using the tests you can both check what you know and increase your knowledge of new concepts and terms in a structured and systematic way.

Nick Brieger

The full series consists of:

Test Your Professional English: Accounting	Alison Pohl
Test Your Professional English: Business General	Steve Flinders
Test Your Professional English: Business Intermediate	Steve Flinders
Test Your Professional English: Finance	Simon Sweeney
Test Your Professional English: Hotel and Catering	Alison Pohl
Test Your Professional English: Law	Nick Brieger
Test Your Professional English: Management	Simon Sweeney
Test Your Professional English: Marketing	Simon Sweeney
Test Your Professional English: Medical	Alison Pohl
Test Your Professional English: Secretarial	Alison Pohl

1 Introduction to law: basic terms

The following terms introduce you to the law and basic legal terminology. Below are the definitions. Find the definition for each term.

authority	court	govern	judge
law enforcement agency	lawyers	legal action	legal system
legislation	rule	the judiciary	~~tribunal~~

1 a body that is appointed to make a judgement or inquiry *tribunal*

2 a country's body of judges ________

3 an act or acts passed by a law-making body ________

4 behaviour recognized by a community as binding or enforceable by authority ________

5 legal proceedings ________

6 an official body that has authority to try criminals, resolve disputes, or make other legal decisions ________

7 an organization responsible for enforcing the law, especially the police ________

8 a senior official in a court of law ________

9 the body or system of rules recognized by a community that are enforceable by established process ________

10 the control resulting from following a community's system of rules ________

11 members of the legal profession ________

12 to rule a society and control the behaviour of its members ________

Lawyer is a wide term which refers to all professionals working in the legal profession; it does not refer to a specific job.

2 Introduction to law: basic concepts

Complete the following text about basic legal concepts using the following words and phrases. Use each term once.

authority	court	govern	judges
law enforcement agency	lawyers	legal action	~~legal systems~~
legislation	rule	the judiciary	tribunal

Why do we have laws and *legal systems* ? At one level, laws can be seen as a type of ______________ which is meant to ______________ behaviour between people. We can find these rules in nearly all social organizations, such as families and sports clubs.

Law, the body of official rules and regulations, generally found in constitutions and ______________ , is used to govern a society and to control the behaviour of its members. In modern societies, a body with ______________ , such as a ______________ or the legislature, makes the law; and a ______________ , such as the police, makes sure it is observed.

In addition to enforcement, a body of expert ______________ is needed to apply the law. This is the role of ______________ , the body of ______________ in a particular country. Of course, legal systems vary between countries, as well as the basis for bringing a case before a court or ______________ . One thing, however, seems to be true all over the world – starting a ______________ is both expensive and time-consuming.

Nouns in English can be divided into countable and uncountable. Countable nouns have a singular and a plural form; uncountable nouns have only one form. **Law** is a countable noun; **legislation** is an uncountable noun.

3 The sources of law

Law has its origins in the early developments of civilized society, and through time there have been major influences on the laws that we follow today.

A Match these sources of law with the descriptions below.

Common law	Roman law
Napoleonic Code	The Ten Commandments

____________________, which evolved in the 8th century BC, was still largely a blend of custom and interpretation by magistrates of the will of the gods.

____________________ evolved from the tribal and local laws in England. It began with common customs, but over time it involved the courts in law-making that was responsive to changes in society. In this way the Anglo-Norman rulers created a system of centralized courts that operated under a single set of laws that replaced the rules laid down by earlier societies.

____________________ formed the basis of all Israelite legislation. They can also be found in the laws of other ancient peoples.

____________________ refers to the entire body of French law, contained in five codes dealing with civil, commercial, and criminal law.

B Are the following sentences about the sources of law true or false?

1 The Ten Commandments are based on moral standards of behaviour.

2 In common law, judges resolve disputes by referring to statutory principles arrived at in advance.

3 Roman law is based on the principle of deciding cases by reference to previous judicial decisions, rather than to written statutes drafted by legislative bodies.

4 The Napoleonic Code was introduced into a number of European countries, notably Belgium, where it is still in force. It also became the model for the civil codes of Quebec Province in Canada, the Netherlands, Italy, Spain, some Latin American republics, and the state of Louisiana.

4 The subject matter of the legal system

A One way of classifying and understanding the law is by subject matter. Lawyers often divide the law and the legal system into two: criminal law and civil law. Classify the following terms into the appropriate column below. Two terms can appear in both columns.

compensation contract crime damages family law
intellectual property ~~plaintiff~~ police private individual
prosecution the accused the defendant theft
to bring a case to bring an action to fine
~~to charge someone with something~~

Criminal	Civil
to charge someone with something	plaintiff

B Now complete the following text contrasting criminal and civil law by choosing from the words/phrases above.

Criminal Law vs Civil Law

One category is the criminal law – the law dealing with ___crime___ . A case is called a ____________ . The case is instituted by the prosecutor, who takes over the case from the ____________ who have already decided ____________ the defendant (or ____________) with specified crimes. The civil law is much more wide-ranging. The civil law includes the law of ____________ and ____________ ____________ . In a civil case, the ____________ , normally a ____________ ____________ or company, ____________ ____________ ____________ to win ____________ . If the case is proven (on the balance of probabilities, meaning that one is more sure than not), the defendant normally pays the plaintiff ____________ (money).

Notice the distinction between **damage** and **damages. Damage** (uncountable singular) refers to physical harm; **damages** (uncountable plural) refers to financial compensation that a person claims for injury or harm that has been suffered.

5 The court structure

Every jurisdiction organizes the administration of justice in different ways. In England, the basic division between criminal and civil law is reflected in the court system. Look at the chart below and then complete the description that refers to each court.

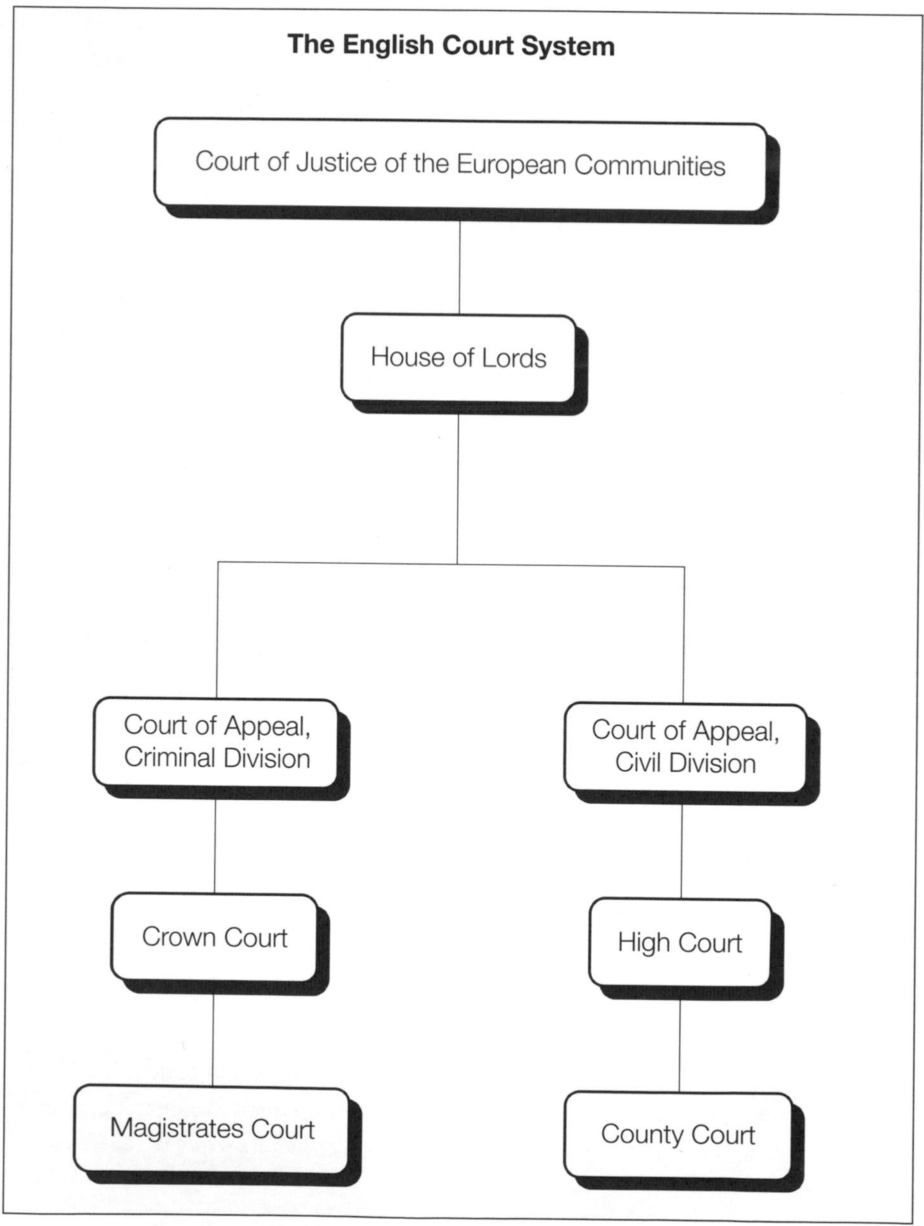

1 Claims of lesser value will start in a County Court . There are 250 of these around the country. They can also deal with divorce and bankruptcy matters.

2 Matters of important legal dispute arising in the Crown Court may be appealed to the ______________ .

3 From the Court of Appeal, there can be an appeal to the ______________ on fact or law, but usually appeal is only allowed on matters of legal importance.

4 If the case involves a serious crime, it is heard in the ______________ (there is only one ______________ but it has about 70 centres around the jurisdiction).

5 In less serious criminal cases (which comprise over 90% of criminal cases), the case is sent for trial in one of over 400 ______________ .

6 More substantial civil claims (over around £25,000) are heard in the ______________ .

7 The ______________ was set up under the Treaty of Rome of 1957, by which the European Community was established. The court can overrule all other courts on matters of Community law.

8 Under the system of appeals in civil cases, it is possible to appeal from a County Court or the High Court to the ______________ .

The judges in the House of Lords are known as Law Lords. They typically sit as a committee to develop and define the law of the land.

6 Court personnel

A Below are 10 people (or groups of people) who work in the different courts. Can you find them in the word square below?

C	J	U	G	U	I	O	P	P	P	P	O	M	T
H	N	O	E	U	Z	V	U	P	L	F	T	N	P
G	L	O	M	C	V	U	Q	J	B	L	R	E	R
N	A	S	A	D	R	T	J	U	D	G	E	N	O
C	H	I	G	E	T	Y	T	R	B	O	C	P	S
J	U	D	I	C	I	A	R	Y	A	S	O	Y	E
P	L	E	S	F	L	E	S	F	T	A	R	Y	C
M	O	L	T	A	X	R	T	E	V	B	D	A	U
A	B	A	R	R	I	S	T	E	R	G	E	L	T
T	E	R	A	A	T	H	I	L	K	G	R	G	O
A	N	O	T	H	E	T	M	P	L	O	X	C	R
A	C	L	E	R	K	M	L	O	I	R	T	U	K
C	H	Y	H	A	N	B	C	T	P	O	L	T	Z
X	P	L	E	P	R	E	S	I	D	E	N	T	A

B Now complete the following text choosing from the words in the square.

The *judiciary* are perhaps the most prominent amongst those involved in running the court. The largest group of ____________ are ____________, ordinary citizens who are not legal professionals but are appointed to ensure that the local community is involved in the running of the legal system. They sit as a group of three (as a '____________'). Magistrates sit with a legally qualified ____________, who can advise on points of law. A case is presented by the ____________, who takes over the case from the police who have already charged the defendant (or accused) with specified crimes.

In the upper courts, the judges are almost all former ____________. But many cases are also heard by ____________ – part-time barristers from private practice. The Crown Court ____________ consists of 12 persons, aged 18 to 70.

The **jury** in an English court is made up of 12 people. Their function is to decide on points of fact, in other words, whether the **accused** committed the crime with which s/he is charged; the role of the **judge** is to advise the jury on points of law.

7 Legal professionals

Every legal system needs professionals to provide legal services. These systems are organized in many different ways. In England this work is carried out by two groups of professionals – solicitors and barristers.

Below is a list of tasks carried out by solicitors and barristers. Classify them into the appropriate column.

advising clients on general legal issues
advising clients on specialist legal issues
advising on litigation
advising on tax matters
~~advocacy in all courts~~
~~advocacy in the lower courts~~
commercial work
conveyancing of houses
dealing with commercial transactions
drafting of documents in connection with litigation
making wills
preparing cases
share and other property dealings

Solicitors	Barristers
advocacy in the lower courts	*advocacy in all courts*

'A **solicitor** is a man who calls in a person he doesn't know to sign a contract he hasn't seen to buy property he doesn't want with money he hasn't got.'

Attributed to: **Dingwall Bateson** (1898–1967), British lawyer

8 Legal training

The legal training for solicitors (who provide general legal advice to clients) and barristers (who present cases in the upper courts) is different. The following short texts describe the stages in legal training, but they are mixed up. Put the steps into the correct category and order.

1 PRACTICE AND CONTINUING EDUCATION
The next stage is to obtain a 'tenancy': becoming an assistant to a practising barrister.

2 GETTING THE QUALIFICATIONS
The next step is to acquire some legal training specific to the work of a barrister.

3 DEVELOPING PRACTICAL SKILLS
Next the intending solicitor has to enter a two-year training contract with a firm of solicitors to gain practical experience in a variety of areas of law.

4 GETTING THE TRAINING AND EXPERIENCE: PUPILLAGE
This is the 'apprenticeship' served by trainee barristers, who are known as pupils. It usually takes a year and consists of a mixture of assisting and observing experienced barristers, as well as more practical experience.

5 GETTING THE ACADEMIC QUALIFICATIONS
The quickest and most common route to qualification is by means of a qualifying law degree.

6 GETTING THE VOCATIONAL QUALIFICATIONS
You will have to undertake the Legal Practice Course, which is the professional training for solicitors. The course teaches the practical application of the law to the needs of clients.

7 GETTING THE ACADEMIC QUALIFICATIONS
The first part of training to become a barrister is known as the academic stage, which provides a general theoretical introduction to the law.

Training for solicitors			**Training for barristers**			
5						

In British English, the noun is spelled **practice** and the verb **practise**; in American English both the noun and the verb are spelled **practise**.

9 Prepositions at law

Every area of English has its own specialist use of prepositions. Law is no exception.

A Below are some typical legal phrases. What preposition do you use with the following phrases?

1 to accuse someone _of_ something
2 to be liable _____ something
3 to sentence someone _____ a punishment
4 to claim damages _____ something
5 to be entitled _____ compensation
6 to bring a case _____ someone
7 to be guilty _____ an offence
8 to fine someone _____ something

B Now complete the following texts with the above phrases. Use each phrase once in the past tense. Write one word in each gap.

1 In Court 1, the Police Prosecutor _accused_ Mary Philips _________ disorderly behaviour. A number of witnesses were called to give evidence. Finally, the magistrate decided that Philips _________ _________ _________ the charge but did not _________ her _________ prison. Instead, he _________ her _________ her behaviour.

2 In Court 2, John Peters _________ _________ _________ _________ his employer. He _________ _________ _________ a serious injury at work. The judge decided that his employer _________ _________ _________ the injury and ruled that Peters _________ _________ _________ substantial damages.

Most words ending in **-ly** are adverbs. However there are some adjectives ending in **-ly**, like **disorderly**.

10 Review test

Now that you have completed section 1, here is a review test to check your knowledge of the terms covered in tests 1–9.

Use the clues on the left to complete the words on the right.

1	a country's body of judges	JUDICIARY
2	senior official in a court of law	_ U _ _ E
3	system of laws which evolved from the tribal and local laws in England	C _ _ M _ _ L _ _
4	system of laws which evolved in the 8th century BC	R _ M _ _ _ A _
5	the branch of law dealing with crime	C _ _ _ I _ A _ L _ _
6	person who institutes a criminal case	P _ _ S _ C _ T _ _
7	person who makes a claim in a civil case	_ L _ _ N _ I _ F
8	the defendant normally pays this to the plaintiff	_ _ M _ G _ S
9	panel of 12 people who decide whether the accused committed a crime	_ _ _ Y
10	lawyer who presents a case to a higher court	_ _ R _ I _ T _ R
11	lawyer who advises clients	_ O _ I _ _ T _ R
12	untrained lawyer who presides over the lowest criminal court	_ A _ _ S _ R _ T _
13	person against whom a civil case is brought	D _ _ E _ D _ _ T
14	an act passed by a law-making body	_ _ G _ S _ A _ I _ _
15	the control resulting from following a community's system of rules	A _ _ H _ R _ _ _
16	'apprenticeship' served by trainee barristers	P _ _ I _ L _ G _
17	becoming an assistant to a practising barrister	T _ _ A _ _ Y
18	court which hears appeals from the Court of Appeal	H _ _ _ E _ F L _ _ _ S

11 Introduction to the law of contract

Here is a brief summary of the law of contract. Complete the texts using the words in the box.

agreement	breach	capacity	consideration	damages	fraud
illegal	~~obligation~~	oral	performance	property	signed	terms

What is a contract?

It is an agreement that creates a binding (1) obligation upon the parties. The essentials of a contract are as follows: mutual (2) ____________ ; a legal (3) ____________ , which in most instances need not be financial; parties who have legal (4) ____________ to make a contract; absence of (5) ____________ or duress; and a subject matter that is not (6) ____________ or against public policy.

What form does a contract take?

In general, contracts may be either (7) ____________ or written. Certain types of contracts, however, in order to be enforceable, must be written and (8) ____________ . These include contracts involving the sale and transfer of (9) ____________ .

How does a contract end?

In case of a (10) ____________ of contract, the injured party may go to court to sue for financial compensation (or (11) ____________), or for rescission, for injunction, or for specific performance if financial compensation would not compensate for the breach. Specific (12) ____________ of a contract is the right by one contracting party to have the other contracting party perform the contract according to the precise (13) ____________ agreed.

Contracts and **agreements** are central to many legal relationships between individuals and between companies and individuals.

12 Types of legal contracts

Link the type of contract to its description.

Type		Description	
1	Consultancy agreement	a	This agreement is used to ensure the repayment of money borrowed, usually in monthly instalments.
2	Distribution agreement	b	This agreement is used where one party buys goods from the manufacturer and re-sells them on his own account. He will however be given the right to use the manufacturer's intellectual property rights.
3	Franchise agreement	c	This agreement sets out the terms and conditions on which a business supplies goods.
4	Loan agreement	d	This agreement is used where one party grants to another the right to run a business in the name of the first party. Examples include Body Shop and McDonalds.
5	Manufacturing licence agreement	e	This is the equivalent of a contract of employment for directors.
6	Terms and conditions of sale agreement	f	This agreement is used where one party is providing services as an independent advisor to a company.
7	Contract of employment	g	This agreement should be used where one party (the licensor) owns intellectual property rights in respect of a product it has developed and wishes to license the manufacture of the product to a third party.
8	Directors' service agreement	h	This is intended to govern the relationship between a number of shareholders in a company. The agreement works as a second layer of protection preventing the company from being run in a manner other than has been agreed.
9	Shareholders' agreement	i	This contract comes into existence as soon as a job offer is accepted whether that offer is oral or in writing.

There are many types of legal contracts which create a legal relationship between individuals and between companies and individuals.

13 Navigating legal contracts

Look at the following extracts from contract clauses. In each, a navigation word has been underlined. Link the underlined word to its meaning.

Contract clauses

1. now it is <u>hereby</u> agreed ....
2. subject as <u>hereinafter</u> provided
3. you will find in the documents <u>herewith</u> attached
4. the first instalment becoming due one month from the date <u>hereof</u>
5. the failure of either party to exercise any right or remedy to which it is entitled <u>hereunder</u>
6. by referring to the points mentioned <u>therein</u>
7. as <u>thereby</u> stated
8. and for a period of 12 months <u>thereafter</u>
9. the failure of either party to exercise any right or remedy shall not constitute a waiver <u>thereof</u>
10. all statutory instruments or orders made pursuant <u>thereto</u>
11. the Initial Fee together with any VAT <u>thereon</u>
12. the cost of the product, and the monthly payments <u>therefore</u>
13. the <u>aforementioned</u> terms shall prevail over ......

Meaning

- a by the terms of this agreement
- b to that thing just mentioned
- c previously stated
- d later in this document
- e after that event
- f by means of this document or declaration
- g in that matter
- h on that item
- i of this event
- j for that item
- k with this document
- l of or about that
- m by means of or because of that

Legal contracts are complex documents. **Drafters** use many specialist legal terms as well as particular words to navigate through the document and relate the different **clauses** together.

14 Standard Terms and Conditions of Sale

Below are the main paragraph titles from a Sale Agreement. Link the paragraph titles to the details of the contents of each paragraph.

1. PRICE AND PAYMENT
2. GOODS
3. DELIVERY
4. ACCEPTANCE
5. TITLE AND RISK
6. LIMITATION OF LIABILITY
7. FORCE MAJEURE
8. ENTIRE AGREEMENT
9. GOVERNING LAW AND JURISDICTION
10. RIGHTS OF CONSUMER

a. The Buyer only receives title to the Goods once he has paid all sums due to the Seller.

b. This prevents a party from relying on something said in pre-contract negotiations that is not excluded in the Agreement itself with the exception of deliberate misrepresentations (which are impossible to exclude).

c. The Goods are as specified in the quotation.

d. Allows for defaults in the event of happenings outside the control of the Seller.

e. The Price is the quoted price; if the Price is not paid on time the Seller is entitled to interest at 4 per cent above base.

f. This does not prevent the buyer suing for breach of warranty after the 7th day. It is intended to prevent rejection.

g. Specifies which law applies and where the parties must sue.

h. Delivery is as shown on the quotation.

i. This is required when selling to consumers. To sell to a consumer without this phrase would be a criminal offence.

j. Tries to exclude and restrict the liability of the Seller to personal injury and death (the minimum allowed by law). It specifically excludes economic loss and limits the liability of the Seller to the price. There is a risk that these terms would be deemed unfair in a consumer transaction.

This document sets out the terms and conditions on which a business supplies goods and is drafted as far as possible to exclude the business's liability for any faulty products. However, statute usually decrees that when a business contracts with a consumer then certain rights cannot be **contracted out of.**

15 Letters of reminder

Collecting unpaid debts requires a mix of tact and persistence. Many companies have to send a stream of reminders before sending the final demand. And it is the last one which usually produces the desired result.

Here are the extracts from three reminders and a final demand. Organize the extracts into the correct letters.

1 We are concerned that this matter is still unresolved and would be grateful to receive your cheque in full settlement of the outstanding sum without further delay.

2 We would like to remind you that the sum of £3500 is still outstanding on your account.

3 Since we have received no replies to our earlier letters, we have no option but to inform you that unless we receive a cheque for the outstanding sum of £3500 within seven days of the date of this letter, we shall place the matter in the hands of our solicitors.

4 I wrote to you on 1st July regarding your unpaid account, amounting to £3500.

5 Clearly, this situation cannot be permitted to continue, and we must urge you to take immediate action to clear the indebtedness.

6 If you are satisfied with the goods supplied to you, we would ask that you kindly settle the account as soon as possible.

7 We have now reminded you twice regarding the outstanding sum of £3500 on your account, but to no avail.

<table>
<tr><th colspan="2">Reminder 1</th><th colspan="2">Reminder 2</th><th colspan="2">Reminder 3</th><th>Final demand</th></tr>
<tr><td>2</td><td></td><td></td><td></td><td></td><td></td><td></td></tr>
</table>

Notice the format for writing dates: **1st July** or **1 July**. However, when we say the date we express it: *the* **1st of July**.

16 Distribution Agreement

Under a Distribution Agreement a distributor buys goods from the manufacturer and re-sells them on his own account. The Definitions Clause of an agreement is usually found at the beginning. It specifies the ways terms are to be understood in the agreement.

Match the following definitions to their descriptions.

DEFINITIONS

1.1 In this Agreement the following expressions shall have the following meanings:

(1) 'the Products'
(2) 'the Trade Mark'
(3) 'the Territory'
(4) 'the Non-Exclusive Territory'
(5) 'the Commencement Date'
(6) 'the Term'

1.2 In addition the following interpretations shall apply:

(7) – the singular shall include the plural and vice versa
(8) – persons shall include corporations, firms and organizations and vice versa
(9) – any gender shall include all genders
(10) – reference to sales and the selling of the Product to customers of the Distributor shall be deemed to include any lease or hire purchase of the same

a name or symbol reserved by a manufacturer to identify their products 2

b the area applicable to the agreement, as described in Part 2 of Schedule 2 ____

c reference to one may mean many ____

d the business relationship may include payment to use the goods as well as payment by instalment for the goods ____

e reference to a person shall include non-persons ____

f reference to male may include female ____

g the goods to be sold by the company ____

h period of time during which the agreement shall remain in force ____

i the time when the agreement shall come into force ____

j the area described in Part 1 of Schedule 2 in which other distributors may be appointed ____

The modal verb **shall** is used in legal contracts and agreements to establish legal obligations. In other words we use **shall** with the meaning of **must**.

17 Franchise Agreement

A franchise is the granting by an individual (the franchisor) to another individual (the franchisee) of the right to run a business in the name of the franchisor. Examples include Body Shop and MacDonalds. Some franchises are exclusive, in other words, no other franchise may be granted in that area. Where the franchise is exclusive the franchisors will want to ensure uniformity with other franchises so that the reputation of the business is not damaged by one particular franchisee. Accordingly, Franchise Agreements tend to be broadly non-negotiable.

Read through Clause 5 on the obligations of the franchisor and then answer the True/False questions below.

5. OBLIGATIONS OF FRANCHISOR

During the Term the Franchisor shall:

5.1. permit the Franchisee to operate the Business and to use the Name and the Marks in accordance with the terms of this Agreement;

5.2. provide the Franchisee with a copy of the Manual and any amendments or updates of the same;

5.3. make available to the Franchisee such services as it makes available to other Franchisees;

5.4. provide the Franchisee with general advice and know-how relating to the Method;

5.5. provide within 30 days of the Commencement Date the Initial Training for the Training Fee;

5.6. within 30 days of the Commencement Date supply the Franchisee with the Equipment at the Equipment Fee;

5.7. not itself operate or grant the right to operate a business in competition with the Business in the Territory;

5.8. update the Manual with any improvements to the Method; and

5.9. keep the Franchisee informed of all relevant legislation

The franchisor		True or False
1	may not allow others to set up a competing business in the same area	True
2	needn't inform the franchisee about new laws	
3	must give the franchisee the operating instructions for the franchise	
4	must allow the franchisee to use any names and trade marks so that the franchisee can develop the business	
5	needn't treat all franchisees in the same way	
6	must train the franchisee in how to operate the business as set out in the instructions	
7	must supply the franchisee with the equipment needed by the business	
8	must send the franchisee all relevant information	

The ending **-or** or **-er** indicates one who grants; **-ee** indicates one who receives. Words using these endings include:
franchisor – franchisee; employer – employee

18 Loan Agreement

Complete the following discussion between a borrower and a lender about setting up a Loan Agreement. The words to complete the conversation are given in the box below.

account	arrears	bank	base rate	capital	conditions
debit	decrease	increase	instalment	interest	loan
payment	penalty	repay	repayment	~~terms~~	

Lender: So, Mr Brown, we are happy to offer you £10,000 on the following (1) ___terms___ .

Mr Brown: Which are?

Lender: Well, if we go through the agreement together I can explain the (2) ____________ .

Mr Brown: OK.

Lender: The (3) ____________ of the loan includes a (4) ____________ repayment of £10,000 plus annual interest at the appropriate rate.

Mr Brown: I see.

Lender: And the (5) ____________ can be repaid over 24 or 36 months.

Mr Brown: Right.

Lender: At present, (6) ____________ on the loan will be calculated at 2% above the bank base rate.

Mr Brown: OK.

Lender: And we will collect the (7) ____________ monthly in (8) ____________ .

Mr Brown: And how will you collect it?

Lender: We will (9) ____________ it directly from your account.

Mr Brown: I see.

Lender: If you agree to the terms, we can arrange to have the money in your (10) ____________ tomorrow. The first repayment (11) ____________ will then be due exactly one month from tomorrow.

Mr Brown: Will the repayment amount be the same each month?

Lender: I'm afraid we can't guarantee that. The exact amount will depend on the (12) ____________. If there is an (13) ____________ , your monthly repayment will go up; if there is a (14) ____________ , it'll go down.

Mr Brown: And what if I want to repay early?

Lender: You can (15) ____________ the loan early but there will be a small (16) ____________ , equal to one month's interest.

- Under a **loan** agreement a **borrower borrows** money from a **lender** at an agreed rate of **interest**. The lender may require some **security** for the loan or not (an **unsecured loan**). The loan is typically repaid in monthly **instalments**.
- Remember that the words **capital** and **interest**, when used in a financial sense, are not used in the plural.

19 Director's Service Agreement

Below are the main paragraph titles from a Director's Service Agreement. Link the paragraph titles to the details of the contents of each paragraph.

1 APPOINTMENT

2 REMUNERATION

3 CONFIDENTIALITY

4 TERMINATION

5 PERIOD OF EMPLOYMENT

6 NOTICE PERIOD

7 HOLIDAYS

8 SICK PAY

9 GRIEVANCE PROCEDURE

10 HOURS OF WORK

11 EXPIRY OF APPOINTMENT

a How the contract may be ended.

b Procedures for handling disagreements.

c Rules about publishing information.

d Rules for payment when the director is away as a result of illness.

e The date when the present contract comes to an end.

f The fixed term of the contract.

g The number of working days when the director can be away from work.

h The pay package.

i The period of advance notice required to terminate the contract.

j This describes the title and general employment of the director.

k When and how the director is expected to discharge his/her work duties/duty.

A **Director's Service Agreement** sets out the terms on which a director is to be appointed. As directors are not employees of the organization, they are typically appointed for a fixed term. The overall terms are usually decided by the Board although directors are not allowed to vote on their own service contract.

20 Consultancy Agreement

Consultants, like directors (see Test 19), are not company employees. A consultant provides services as an independent advisor to a company. A Consultancy Agreement is drafted from the company's perspective and sets out the obligations of the consultant.

The clause dealing with 'duties' is central to the agreement. Below are extracts from this clause. Each missing word is derived from the word in brackets.

DUTIES

2.1 Subject as hereinafter ___provided___ (provision) and except at such times as the Consultant may be incapacitated by ____________ (ill) or accident, the Consultant shall devote such of his time, ____________ (attentive) and skill as may be necessary for the proper discharge of his duties, save that nothing in this Agreement shall require the Consultant to devote to his ____________ (oblige) under this Agreement more than 60 hours ____________ (month).

2.2 The Consultant shall keep the Board of Directors of the Company ('the Board') ____________ (information) of progress on projects in which the Consultant is engaged and shall produce ____________ (write) reports on the same from time to time when so ____________ (request) by the Board. While the Consultant's method of work is his own, he shall comply with the ____________ (reason) requests of the Board and shall work and co-operate with any ____________ (serve) or agent or other consultant of the Company.

2.3 The Consultant will not during his ____________ (engage) [and for a period of twelve months thereafter] undertake any ____________ (add) activities or accept other engagements which would ____________ (interference) with or preclude the ____________ (perform) of his duties under this Agreement or which lead to or might lead to any conflict of ____________ (interesting) between the Consultant and the best interests of the Company.

Notice the following words of frequency:

daily hourly monthly quarterly weekly yearly/annually

All these words can be used as adjectives and adverbs, except *annually* which is only an adverb.

21 Full-time Employment Contract

A contract of employment comes into existence as soon as a job offer is accepted whether that offer is oral or in writing. However, it is easier for both parties if the offer of employment is in writing to prevent disputes at a later date.

Below is an extract from a skeleton contract of employment for a full-time employee. The key word/phrase from each section has been removed. Complete the text using the words/phrases from the box.

commencing salary · date of commencement · duties and responsibilities · grievance · holiday entitlement · notice · pension · ~~position~~ · probationary service · sickness pay · terms and conditions

1 You have been appointed to the *position* of administrative assistant.

2 Your ______________ will be as detailed in the attached Job Description, but this Job Description should not be regarded as exclusive or exhaustive. There will be other occasional duties and requirements associated with your appointment.

3 The ______________ of your continuous service with this company is 1 January 2002.

4 Your specific ______________ are contained in the Employees' Handbook issued by the company, as well as in existing collective agreements negotiated by this company.

5 Confirmation of your appointment will be subject to your satisfactory completion of 3 months' ______________ .

6 Your ______________________ is £20,000 per annum, paid monthly in arrears. Overtime is not payable.

7 Your ______________________ entitlement is 30 days in any calendar year.

8 Your annual ______________________ is 25 days which cannot be carried over.

9 The minimum period of ______________________ to which you are entitled is 3 months.

10 Your position with regard to ______________________ is set out in the explanatory booklet attached.

11 If you have a ______________________ relating to your employment, you should refer to the complaints procedure outlined in the booklet attached.

There are no fixed rules for combining nouns. Here are the options:
Saxon genitive, for example **employees' handbook**
prepositional phrase, for example **confirmation of your appointment**
noun + noun, for example **job description**

22 Verbal and written warnings

Below are some comments from bosses in disciplinary interviews and some extracts from written warnings. Match each reason for the warning with an item from each box.

Reason for the warning								
Poor work	6	d	Poor attitude			Delay		
Behaviour			Punctuality			Housekeeping		

Comments from interviews

1 You've been late twice this week. I talked to you before about this and made clear, I hope, that this is not acceptable.

2 I am sure that I don't need to remind you that we agreed that the report would be ready by Friday afternoon. I am disappointed that the deadline came and went without any sign of the report and no explanation from you.

3 We cannot accept rudeness from any of our employees. I don't just mean with customers, but with colleagues and suppliers.

4 We have noticed that you just don't seem interested in your work. This creates a bad atmosphere in the office.

5 The PCs were left on again yesterday. Please make sure that this doesn't happen again.

6 In general I have to tell you that I am not satisfied with your work. I have also had a number of comments from other members of staff that you are not doing the work to the standard that we expect.

Written warning

a I understand from Patrick Standish that you were rude when dealing with a customer. I must emphasize that I shall not hesitate to take disciplinary action against you in the event of any recurrence.

b Despite my instructions to the contrary, you are failing to arrive punctually for work. I find it annoying and disappointing that I should be required to write this. Please understand that if this continues it will certainly result in disciplinary action being taken against you.

c Despite specific office instructions to the contrary, some of you are failing to switch off your computer equipment before leaving the office at the end of the day. Quite apart from aspects of security, such careless habits reflect badly on the department as a whole, and the individuals concerned in particular.

d I wish to draw your attention to the manner in which you are currently dealing with your responsibilities as sales rep.

e I must emphasize that this is just not acceptable, and I require you to bring about an immediate and marked improvement in your attitude.

f Since I have heard nothing from you, I am forced to assume that there are no reasons for this delay – and I find this most disappointing. Please ensure that the completed document is with me by Monday morning.

A **warning** can serve as the basis for a **disciplinary interview**, which can, in turn, lead to **dismissal**. There are many **grounds** on which an employer can **sack** an employee. To be fair, however, she needs to explain the reason for dissatisfaction and give the employee an opportunity to improve.

23 Letter of redundancy

Making an employee redundant is one of the tougher tasks. So it needs to be done with care and sensitivity.

Below is a letter of redundancy. The sentences have been mixed up. Put them into order.

1 Details of your forthcoming redundancy and severance pay are enclosed.

2 Finally, I shall, of course, be only too pleased to supply any prospective employer with a reference on your behalf.

3 I am writing in connection with our discussion of earlier today.

4 Yours sincerely
Anne O'Dwyer
Personnel Manager

5 It is with much regret that I must ask you to accept this letter as formal notice of the redundancy of your position as administrative assistant with effect from 30 September 2001.

6 Dear Ms Bailey

7 On behalf of the Company, I would like to thank you for the services you have given us in the past and wish you every success in the future.

8 Please do not hesitate to contact me if you need clarification.

9 The Company will gladly grant you reasonable time off with pay for the purposes of attending job interviews or undertaking any training for alternative employment.

10 The services of the Personnel Department will, of course, be freely available to assist you in obtaining suitable alternative employment.

6									

The normal conventions of greetings and farewells in letters are:

Dear Ms Bailey (named addressee)	**Yours sincerely**
Dear Sirs (unnamed addressee)	**Yours faithfully**

We normally use the name of the addressee if we know it.

24 Employment discrimination

Many countries have employment legislation which prohibits discrimination against employees. As we shall see, a number of discriminatory practices have been banned. These include bias in:

- hiring
- promotion
- termination
- compensation
- job assignment
- various types of harassment

Below are some key grounds on which bias in employment is specifically outlawed. Link the ground with its description.

Grounds	Description
1 race	a Where the job applicant will give birth in the near future.
2 sex	b Where the candidate comes from a country in the developing world.
3 religion	c Where the person is over 40.
4 colour	d Where the employee is homosexual.
5 national origin	e Where the prospective employee is a woman.
6 physical disability	f Where the employee has a young family.
7 age	g Where the employee belongs to a lesser known sect.
8 pregnancy	h Where the applicant is dark-skinned.
9 childbirth	i Where the employee has been sick as a result of pregnancy.
10 medical conditions related to childbirth	j Where the applicant has a bodily handicap, but will still be able to perform the job.
11 sexual orientation	k Where the candidate is non-European.

25 Employment law and Human Resource terms

This crossword has terms taken from a wide area of legal and Human Resource areas.

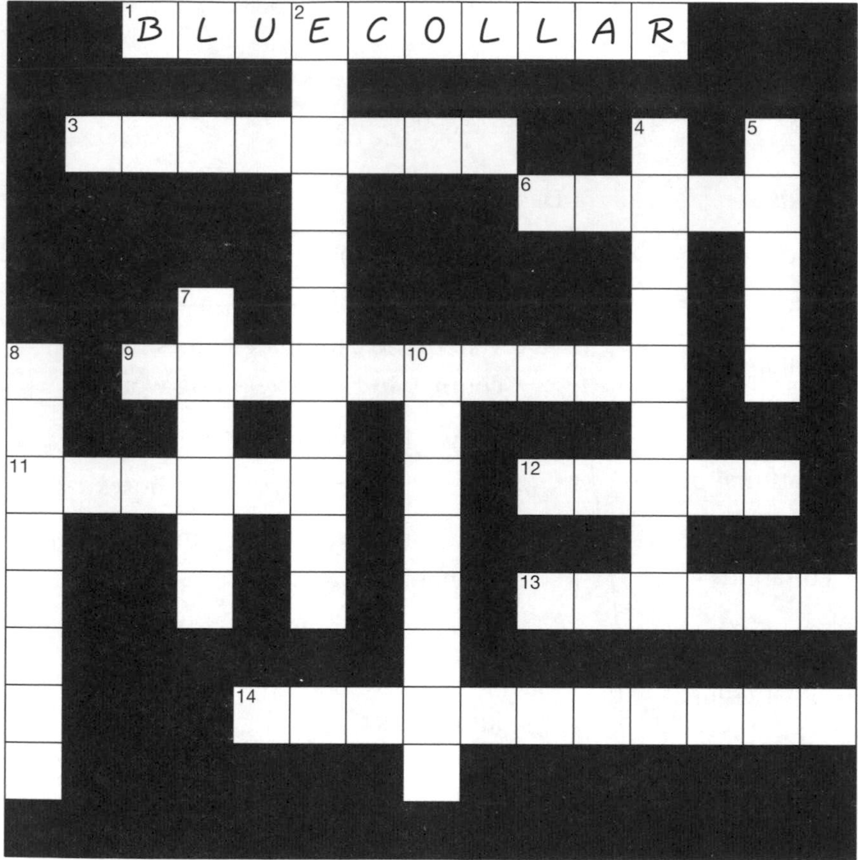

Across

1 Someone who works in a manual job or in a job on the factory floor.

3 When you work only part of the standard working week.

6 The level of a job within the structure of a company's workforce.

9 Someone in charge of several other (usually blue-collar) workers.

11 Advance information.

12 A system of working where one group of workers starts work as soon as the other group finishes.

13 A day when you do not go to work. (2 words)

14 Someone who is below you in the organization.

Down

2 Your rights, e.g. to holidays.

4 A type of leave that women take when they have a baby.

5 Holiday or permission to be away from work.

7 The different parts of the job that you will have to do.

8 The total of all people who work in a company.

10 A period of time when you do not have to go to work.

In a corporate setting, the Human Resources (HR) Department is concerned with different aspects of the employees' terms and conditions of employment. These range from **recruitment** and **selection** through to **health**, **safety** and **environment**.

26 Employee health and safety

The following text deals with aspects of employee health and safety. Complete the gaps with an appropriate word derived from the words given.

Workplace (1) safety (safe) and (2) ______________ (healthy) laws establish basic standards aimed at reducing the number of (3) ______________ (ill), (4) ______________ (injure) and (5) ______________ (die) in workplaces. Because most workplace safety (6) ______________ (regulate) rely for their effectiveness on employees who are willing to report job (7) ______________ (dangerous), most laws also prevent employers from firing or discriminating against employees who report (8) ______________ (safe) conditions to proper authorities.

Workers' compensation laws are designed to ensure that employees who are (9) ______________ (injure) or (10) ______________ (disable) on the job are provided with fixed (11) ______________ (money) awards, eliminating the need for litigation. These laws also provide benefits for (12) ______________ (depend) of those (13) ______________ (work) who are killed because of work-related accidents or illnesses. Some laws also provide (14) ______________ (protect) for employers and fellow workers by limiting the amount an injured employee can (15) ______________ (recovery) from an employer and by eliminating the (16) ______________ (liable) of co-workers in most accidents.

In recent years, workers in many countries have pushed strongly for laws to protect their health and safety on the job. In many cases they have been somewhat successful.

27 Introduction to criminal law

A criminal is someone who commits a crime. Below are 12 phrases using the word *criminal*. Link each phrase to its definition.

Phrase	Definition
1 Court of Criminal Appeal	a a barrister or solicitor who specializes in felonies and misdemeanours
2 criminal contempt	b a person charged with or convicted of crimes against humanity
3 criminal negligence	c previous crimes of which an individual has been convicted
4 criminal court	d rules governing the investigation of crimes; the arrest, charging, and trial of accused criminals; and the sentencing of those convicted (found guilty of a crime)
5 criminal forfeiture	e one of the higher courts of law which hears cases sent up for review
6 criminal law	f disorderly behaviour, disrespect, or disobedience of a judge's orders, particularly during a trial
7 criminal lawyer	g a person who repeatedly commits offences
8 criminal procedure	h where an individual fails to exercise a duty of care and the resulting action leads to the commission of a crime
9 criminal record	i the branch of law which deals with felonies and misdemeanours
10 habitual criminal	j study of the mental processes and behaviour of persons who commit crimes
11 criminal liability	k a court with jurisdiction to hear felonies and misdemeanours
12 war criminal	l responsibility for committing a crime (excluded persons include minors and the insane)

A **crime** is any act or omission (of an act) that violates the law and is punishable by the state. Crimes are considered injurious to society or the community. They include both **felonies** (more serious offences – like **murder** or **rape**) and **misdemeanours** (like **petty theft**, or **speeding**).

28 Types of crime

Below are 14 crimes. Firstly, link each crime to its definition and then classify each crime as violent (V) or non-violent (NV).

V or NV	Name of crime	Definition of crime
	assault	a generic term for the killing of another person
	drug dealing	any instance in which one party deceives or takes unfair advantage of another
V	money laundering	attempt to use illegal force on another person
	battery	attempt to use illegal force on another person in the absence of consent to sexual relations
	homicide	attempt to transform illegally acquired money into apparently legitimate money
	manslaughter	driving a vehicle in excess of the permitted limit
	fraud	leaving one's vehicle in an area or for a duration in contravention of the law
	murder	possession of and/or trading in illegal substances
	armed robbery	taking the property of another without right or permission
	sexual assault	the actual use of illegal force on another person
	burglary	the crime of breaking into a private home with the intention of committing a felony
	theft	the unlawful killing of a person with intent
	parking	the unlawful killing of a person without malicious intent and therefore without premeditation
	speeding	the unlawful taking of another's property using a dangerous weapon

29 Criminal procedure (1)

Put the following stages into the correct sequence in the flowchart below.

acquittal of accused	conviction of accused
appeal against judgement	interrogation of witnesses
appearance in court	~~investigation by police~~
apprehension of suspect	release on bail
charge of suspect	sentence by judge

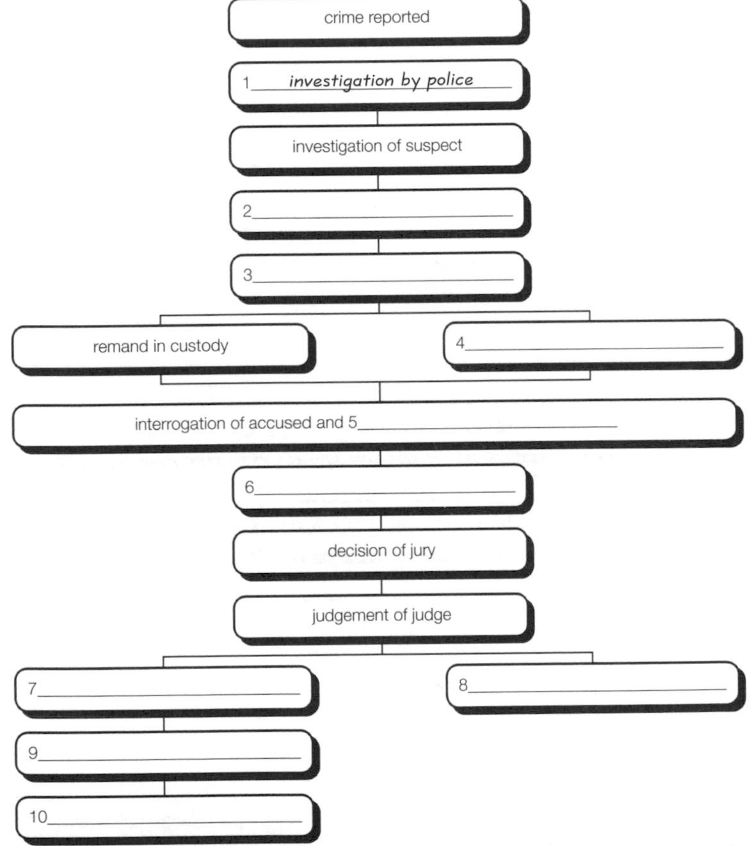

The law of criminal procedure regulates the modes of **apprehending**, **charging**, and **trying** suspected offenders; the imposition of **penalties** on convicted offenders; and the methods of challenging the legality of **conviction** after judgement is entered.

30 Criminal procedure (2)

In the previous test we looked at the typical stages in criminal procedure. In this test, we will look at what happens at each stage. Below is the completed flowchart of the criminal procedure. Match each step to its correct definition.

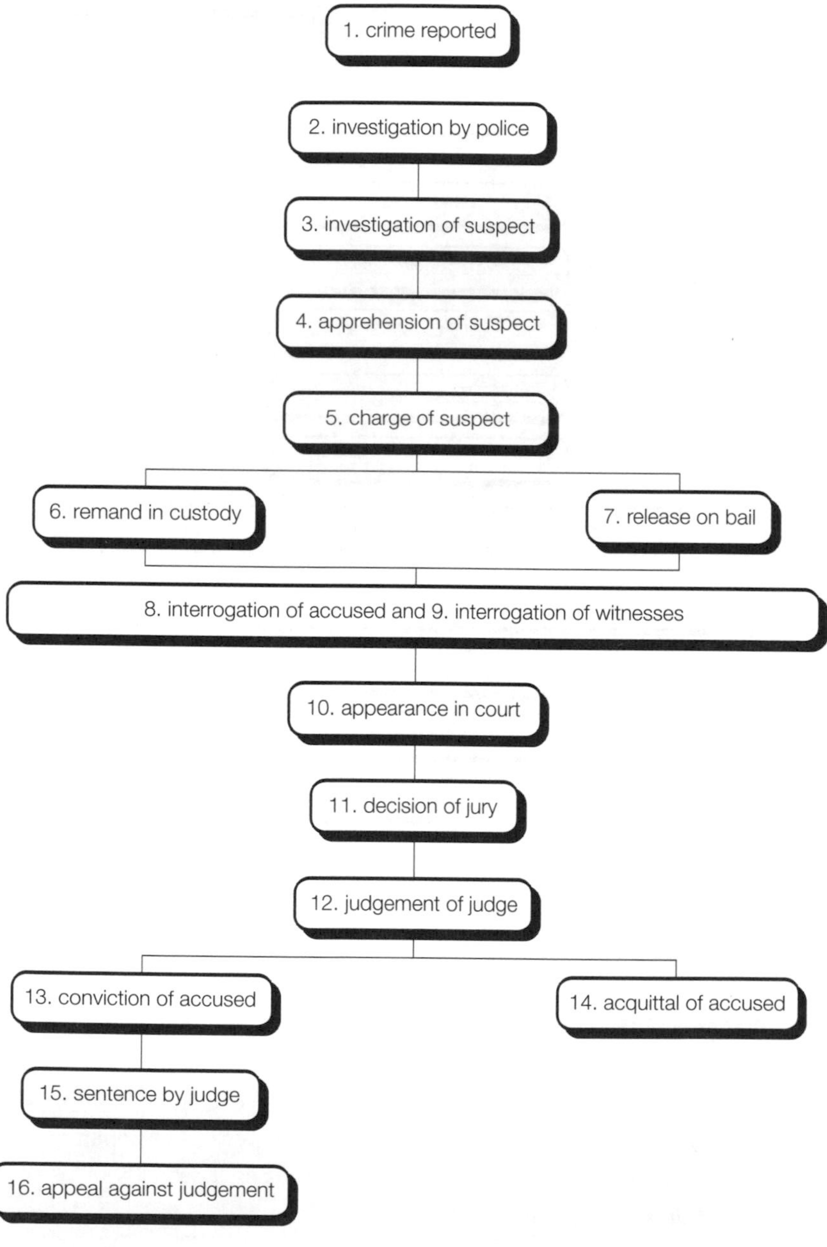

a ___7___: the police free the person alleged to have committed the crime on condition that the accused appears at court at a future date

b _________: the jury panel make a decision whether they believe (beyond reasonable doubt) that the accused committed the crime of which s/he is accused

c _________: the judge decides punishment

d _________: the police carry out a systematic examination of the person who may have committed a crime

e _________: the police receive information that a crime may have been committed

f _________: the police make a claim of wrongdoing against the person alleged to have committed the crime

g _________: the police carry out further questioning of the person alleged to have committed the crime

h _________: the defendant is found not guilty of the charge

i _________: the accused comes to court to face charges

j _________: the police carry out a detailed enquiry into the alleged crime

k _________: after being found guilty, the accused brings an action to clear his/her name or to reduce the sentence

l _________: the police arrest the person who is alleged to have committed the crime

m _________: the police detain the person alleged to have committed the crime

n _________: the judge makes a judicial decision

o _________: the police collect evidence against the accused from those who can give evidence

p _________: the defendant is found guilty

31 Sentencing

Below is a range of sentences that may be imposed. Match each sentence to its definition.

Sentence

1 bond
2 capital punishment
3 jail
4 parole
5 imprisonment
6 probation
7 concurrent sentence
8 binding over
9 suspended sentence
10 peace bond
11 community service
12 determinate sentence
13 prison
14 good behaviour

Definition

a When two or more terms of imprisonment are served together.

b A place for long-term incarceration for a crime.

c A place of confinement for time periods longer than those usual for a police station lock-up and shorter than those usual for a prison.

d Unpaid work undertaken pursuant to a court order upon conviction for an offence in lieu of a sentence of imprisonment.

e A release from prison, before a sentence is finished, that depends on the person 'keeping clean' and doing what he or she is supposed to do while out. If the person fails to meet the conditions, the rest of the sentence must be served.

f Conduct required for criminals to get out of jail early or other privileges while in prison.

- g A sentence (usually 'jail time') that the judge allows the convicted person to avoid serving (e.g. if the person continues on good behaviour, completes community service, etc.).
- h A document that promises to pay money if a particular future event happens, or a sum of money that is put up and will be lost if that event happens.
- i An act by which the court requires a bond or bail money.
- j The sentencing of a criminal to a period of time during which they will be deprived of their freedom.
- k A bond, required by a judge of a person likely to 'breach the peace', to guarantee the person's good behaviour for a period of time.
- l An exact prison term that is set by law, rather than one that may be shortened for good behaviour.
- m A kind of punishment given out as part of a sentence, which means that instead of jailing a person convicted of a crime, a judge will order that the person reports to an officer regularly and according to a set schedule.
- n The most severe of all sentences: that of death. Also known as the death penalty.

1	2	3	4	5	6	7	8	9	10	11	12	13	14
h													

In countries following the Anglo-American legal tradition, **sentencing** is a function that is distinguished from that of determining **guilt** or **innocence** and is normally the responsibility of the judge rather than of the jury. Systems of law traditionally give the judge a wide discretion in determining both the kind of **penalty** to be imposed (**imprisonment**, **fine**, **probation**) and its extent. As modern sentencing systems provide an increasingly wide range of forms of sentence, the choice of sentence becomes a more complex task.

32 At trial

The climax of the legal proceedings is the trial. Read the following text about the trial and the answer the true/false questions below the text.

A trial may be defined broadly and comprehensively as a judicial examination of the issues between the parties. Although some variations may exist, trials are usually held before a judge sitting alone, a referee, or a judge and jury. The counsels for the prosecution and for the defence make opening statements to the jury, outlining what each sees as the nature of the case and what each hopes to prove as the trial proceeds. Next, the counsel for the prosecution presents his case by calling witnesses, questioning them, and permitting them to be cross-examined by the counsel for the defence. The counsel for each side then makes a closing argument to the jury, summarizing the evidence in a light most favourable to their respective clients. The function of the jury is to determine the facts of the case, whereas the function of the judge is to determine the applicable law and to oversee the parties' presentation of the facts to the court. After the judge has instructed the jury on the applicable law, the jury will retire to deliberate in private until it reaches a just verdict, which will then be announced in open court. The verdict of a jury terminates the trial. In a case tried before a judge sitting alone, the decision of the judge constitutes a termination of the trial.

1	Criminal trials are always held in front of a jury.	False
2	A judge may sit alone to hear a legal case.	_______
3	At the beginning of the trial both counsels outline their case.	_______
4	The counsel for the defence may cross-examine prosecution witnesses.	_______
5	The function of the jury is to decide the applicable law.	_______
6	The judge may intervene if the counsels on either side fail to observe the court procedures.	_______
7	The judge advises the jury on the law relevant to the case.	_______
8	The jury discusses their verdict in open court.	_______

Legal procedures and the role of the judge vary in different jurisdictions. In an **adversarial** system, the parties are **cross-examined** in order to find out the truth; the judge is an impartial referee. In an **inquisitorial** system, the judge plays a more proactive role, asking questions in order to find out the truth.

33 Key players in the criminal law

A number of agencies, organizations and individuals are involved in the administration of the criminal law. The most important are:

- the police
- the suspect
- the jury
- the magistrate
- the defence counsel
- the prosecutor
- the judge

Draw lines to combine the two halves of the sentences to describe the functions of each.

Who	**What**
The police interrogate	arrests, searches, and seizures.
The police carry out	on the sentence to be imposed.
The magistrate sometimes conducts	over the court.
The prosecutor conducts	suspects and witnesses.
The suspect has the right	the case in court on behalf of the police.
The suspect is innocent	the investigation in cases of serious criminal offence.
The defence counsel assists	the suspect from violations of his rights at the hands of law-enforcement personnel.
The defence counsel protects	the suspect in gathering exonerating evidence.
The judge presides	to remain silent.
The judge decides	until proved guilty.
The jury decides	whether the accused is guilty or not.

Collective nouns such as **police** can be used either in the singular or the plural. In other words we can say both:

*the **police** interrogate …*

*the **police** interrogates …*

We use the noun in a plural form when we view them as a group of individuals; we use the noun in the singular form when we view them as a single collective entity.

34 On appeal

A Below are some words and phrases derived from 'appeal'. Link each item to its definition.

Word/expression	Definition
1 appeal	a Permission of the court to institute appeal proceedings from a single judge or lower court to a full court or higher court respectively.
2 appellate	b The person against whom an appeal is taken (usually, but not always, the winner in the lower court).
3 appealable	c To ask a more senior court or person to review a decision of a subordinate court or person.
4 leave to appeal	d A court to which appeals are made on points of law resulting from the judgement of a lower court.
5 appellant	e Describes a judgement which can be appealed against.
6 court of appeal	f Money put up by someone appealing a court's decision. This money is to pay the other side's costs in case the person appealing fails to go forward with an honest appeal.
7 appellee	g A party who appeals against a judicial decision which is not in that party's favour.
8 appeal bond	h Refers to a higher court that can hear appeals from a lower court.

B Now complete the following text about appellate procedure using the words/expressions above.

___Appellate___ procedure consists of the rules and practices by which a ____________________ reviews trial court judgements. The procedure focuses on several main themes:

- what judgements are ____________________ ,
- how an ____________________ is to be brought before the court,
- what will be required for a reversal of the lower court,
- what procedures the parties must follow

Often an ____________________ will be put up to pay the other side's costs in case the appeal fails.

Normally ____________________ will be requested by the ____________________ , who is seeking a review of the decision of a subordinate court or person. The other party, the ____________________ , is usually, but not always, the winner in the lower court.

An **appeal** is the transfer of a case from a lower to a higher court for a new **hearing** in order to reverse the decision made by the lower court. **Procedure** consists of the rules and practices by which the higher courts review trial court judgements.

35 Branches of civil law

While criminal law regulates those acts or omissions that are considered injurious to the state or to society, civil law aims to regulate relations between individuals or between individuals and organizations. There are many branches of civil law, some of which we will explore in this section.

Match the subject areas in the box with the branches of law below.

Agriculture	Civil Rights	Divorce	Environmental Law
Foreign Relations Law	Joint Ventures	Landlord–Tenant	
Pensions	~~Product Liability~~	Property Tax	Unfair Competition

Areas	**Branches**
Product Liability	Accident and Injury Compensation and Prevention
	Constitutional Law, Individual Rights
	Employment Law
	Enterprise Law
	Family Law
	Intellectual Property
	International, Transnational, Comparative Law
	Law relating to Commercial Transactions
	Law relating to Particular Activities/Business Sectors
	Property, Natural Resources, the Environment
	Taxation

36 Law of Commercial Transactions

There are many commercial relationships which are established by people in the world of business. These relationships will typically be regulated by a body of law. Brought together, these branches of law represent the law of commercial transactions.

Below are the main areas of commercial law. Match each branch to the contents it covers.

~~Banking~~ Bankruptcy Commercial Law Consumer Credit
Contracts Debtor and Creditor Landlord and Tenant
Mortgages Negotiable Instruments Real Estate Transactions
Sales Secured Transactions

1 These regulations establish which institutions may offer credit and debit facilities. Banking

2 This law provides for the development of a plan that allows a debtor, who is unable to pay his creditors, to resolve his debts through the division of his assets among his creditors. ______

3 This branch of law governs the broad areas of business, commerce, and consumer transactions. ______

4 This law regulates how consumers may finance transactions without having to pay the full cost of the merchandise at the time of the transaction. ______

5 This law covers promises that the law will enforce. It provides remedies if a promise is breached. ______

6 This law governs situations where one party is unable to pay a monetary debt to another. ____________

7 This law governs the rental of commercial and residential property. The basis of the legal relationship between the parties is grounded in both contract and property law. ____________

8 This transaction involves the transfer of an interest in land as a security for a loan or other obligation. It is the most common method of financing real estate transactions. ____________

9 These are 'unconditioned writings' that promise or order the payment of a fixed amount of money. Drafts and notes are the two main categories. ____________

10 The agreement to sell between a buyer and seller is governed by the general principles of contract law. It is normally required that these types of contract be in writing. ____________

11 This branch of law regulates every phase of a transaction for the sale of goods and provides remedies for problems that may arise. It provides for implied warranties of merchantability and fitness. ____________

12 This interest arises when in exchange for a type of loan a borrower agrees, in a security agreement, that a lender (the secured party) may take specified collateral owned by the borrower if he should default on the loan. ____________

Notice the pronunciation of **debt** and **debtor**. In both cases the *b* is silent. However, in **debit** the *b* is pronounced.

Underline the silent letters in the following words:

bankruptcy **mortgage**

37 Agency agreements

Below are seven agency relationships in the columns labelled Terms (1) and Terms (2). Match the principals from Terms (1) with the agents from Terms (2). Finally, match each term with its definition in the columns labelled Definitions (1) and Definitions (2).

Terms (1)	Terms (2)	Definitions (1)	Definitions (2)
attorney	beneficiary	one that hires others to perform a service or engage in an activity in exchange for compensation	a person entitled to receive under the terms of a will
executor	client	an officer appointed by the shareholders to represent their interests	a person who by reason of incapacity is under the control of another
trustee	employee	an individual who, by legal appointment or by the effect of a written law, is given custody of both the property and the person of one who is unable to manage his own affairs, such as a child or mentally-disabled person	a person who serves others
master	heir	an individual or entity (as a corporation) having control or authority over another	a person hired by another to perform a service especially for wages or salary and who is under the other's control
guardian	servant	a person specifically appointed by a testator to administer the will ensuring that final wishes are respected (i.e. that the will is properly 'executed')	a person or entity named or otherwise entitled to receive the principal or income or both from a trust
corporate director	stockholder	a person authorized to act on another's behalf as a lawyer	a person who buys the services of another, in this case legal services
employer	ward	a natural or legal person to whom property is committed to be administered for the benefit of a beneficiary (as a person or charitable organization)	an owner of corporate stock

Enterprise law includes the **financing**, **formation**, and **regulation** of business and non-profit entities. One branch is agency law which is concerned with any **principal–agent** relationship: a relationship in which one person has legal authority to act for another. Such relationships arise from explicit appointment, or by implication.

38 Law of Property, Natural Resources, the Environment

The main objective of this area of law is to ensure that the environment is protected against both public and private actions that fail to take account of costs or harm inflicted on the eco-system.

A The major concerns are listed in two columns. Match a word on the left with one on the right to form 13 phrases related to the law of property.

atomic	waters
clean	water
clean	species
endangered	sources
energy	resources
natural	pollution
navigable	pollution
noise	forests
ocean	energy
oil	dumping
pesticide	disposal
tropical	control
waste	air

B Now answer the following sentences using the appropriate phrase from the above list.

1. Which legislation prevents the destruction of large areas of trees in the equatorial areas?
2. Which legislation protects the quality of the water that we drink?
3. Which legislation controls the application of chemicals in farming?
4. Which legislation prevents the disposal of rubbish at sea?
5. Which legislation protects our ears?
6. Which legislation protects those animals which are in danger of extinction?

39 Intellectual Property

Intellectual Property Law is designed to promote the worldwide protection of both industrial property (inventions, trademarks, and designs) and copyright materials (literary, musical, photographic, and other artistic works).

The following crossword contains key words from this branch of law.

Across

1 New.

3 Wrongful.

7 For a _________ period of time, i.e. fixed.

10 Person who creates something new.

12 Permitted only to authorized people.

15 Writer.

16 The protection granted to authors.

17 Permitted.

Down

2 Not existing before, different from others.

4 What the person wishing to protect their interest applies for.

5 A breach of copyright, etc.

6 To find out something new.

8 What you must do if you want your intellectual property to be protected.

9 Distinctive symbol, picture or word.

11 What an author produces.

13 The right given to an inventor.

14 The law aims to _________ authors, patent holders, etc.

40 Family Law

Below are the main areas that Family Law covers. The text gives excerpts from those areas. Write one area above each text.

~~Adoption~~	Estate Planning
Child Custody	Estates and Trusts
Children's Rights	Insurance
Divorce	Marriage

1 Adoption

The process by which a legal parent–child relationship is created between individuals not biologically parent and child.

2 ____________________

The parents of a child born within a marriage are joint guardians of that child and the rights of both parents are equal.

3 ____________________

Children are generally afforded the basic rights embodied by the constitution.

4 ____________________

As a result of this both parties' status becomes single again.

5 ____________________

The process by which an individual or family arranges the transfer of assets in anticipation of death.

6 ____________________

Generally, a trust is a right in property (real or personal) which is held in a fiduciary relationship by one party for the benefit of another. The trustee is the one who holds title to the trust property, and the beneficiary is the person who receives the benefits of the trust.

7 ____________________

While types vary widely, their primary goal is to allocate the risks of a loss from the individual to a great number of people.

8 ____________________

A contract based upon a voluntary private agreement by a man and a woman to become husband and wife.

Family law is the body of law which regulates **family relationships**, including **marriage** and **divorce**, the treatment of children, and money issues.

41 Accident and Injury: Compensation and Prevention

Accidents can happen in a variety of situations. Where there is a duty of care, then the injured party has grounds for a claim. Modern insurance practice makes it easier to satisfy the injured without financially crushing the injurer.

This area of law covers a number of different aspects:

- Damages
- Insurance
- Product Liability
- Torts and Personal Injury
- Workers' Compensation

Read through the short texts below and then answer the questions.

1 Damages, in a legal sense, are the sum of money the law imposes for a breach of some duty or violation of some right. Generally, there are two types of damages: compensatory and punitive. The former are intended to compensate the injured party for his loss or injury; the latter are awarded to punish a wrongdoer.

---

2 In the absence of insurance, three possible individuals bear the burden of an economic loss: the individual suffering the loss; the individual causing the loss via negligence or unlawful conduct; or a particular party who has been allocated the burden by the legislature, such as employers under Workers' Compensation statutes.

---

3 Product liability refers to the liability of any or all parties along the chain of manufacture of any product for damage caused by that product. This includes the manufacturer of component parts (at the top of the chain), an assembling manufacturer, the wholesaler, and the retail store owner (at the bottom of the chain). Products containing inherent defects that cause harm to a consumer of the product, or someone to whom the product was loaned or given, are the subjects of product liability suits.

---

4 Torts are civil wrongs that are recognized by law as grounds for a lawsuit. These wrongs result in an injury or harm which constitutes the basis for a claim by the injured party. The injured person may sue for an injunction to prevent the continuation of the tortious conduct or for monetary damages. Among the types of damages the injured party may recover are: loss of earning capacity, pain and suffering, and reasonable medical expenses. They include both present and future expected losses.

---

5 Workers' Compensation laws are designed to ensure that employees who are injured or disabled on the job are provided with fixed monetary awards, eliminating the need for litigation. These laws also provide benefits for dependants of those workers who are killed because of work-related accidents or illnesses. Some laws also protect employers and fellow workers by limiting the amount an injured employee can recover from an employer and by eliminating the liability of co-workers in most accidents.

---

1 What are the two types of damages? What is the difference between them?

2 When there is no insurance, who may have to bear the loss?

3 What are the parties along the chain of manufacture?

4 What remedies are open to the injured party in a tort case?

5 Who can benefit from Workers' Compensation laws?

42 Introduction to company law

The following text introduces the area of company law. Complete the text by using the words in the box below.

agreements borrow corporations court debts dividends employees ~~legal~~ legislation liability limited objectives partnership profits property registered (x2) shareholders sole trader sue

A company is a ___legal___ entity, allowed by __________ , which permits a group of people, as __________ , to create an organization, which can then focus on pursuing set __________ . It is empowered with legal rights which are usually only reserved for individuals, such as the right to __________ and be sued, own __________ , hire __________ or loan and __________ money. The primary advantage of a company structure is that it provides the shareholders with a right to participate in the __________ , a proportionate distribution of profits made in the form of a money payment to shareholders, without any personal __________ .

There are various forms of legal business entities ranging from the __________ , who alone bears the risk and responsibility of running a business, taking the profits, but as such not forming any association in law and thus not regulated by special rules of law, to the __________ company with __________ liability and to multinational __________ .

In a __________ , members 'associate', forming collectively an association in which they all participate in management and sharing __________ , bearing the liability for the firm's __________ and being sued jointly and severally in relation to the firm's contracts or tortious acts.

Limited-liability companies, or corporations, unlike partnerships, are formed not simply by __________ entered into between their first members; they must also be __________ at a public office or __________ designated by law or otherwise obtain official acknowledgement of their existence.

43 Registration of new companies

Match the following titles from the regulations for registration to the extracts from the details.

Titles

1 What are articles of association? ___c___

2 Can anyone be a company director? ______

3 What company types are there? ______

4 What is the minimum number of officers a company requires? ______

5 Who can form a company? ______

6 Can I choose any name I want for my company? ______

7 How do I form a company? ______

8 What is a registered office? ______

9 What is a memorandum of association? ______

Extracts from the details

a One or more persons but a public company or an unlimited company must have at least two subscribers.

b It is the address of a company to which Companies House letters and reminders will be sent.

c This document sets out the rules for running the company's internal affairs.

d By sending a memorandum of association, the articles of association, the details of the directors and the company secretary, and a statement of legal compliance.

e On condition that you are not:

- an undischarged bankrupt or disqualified by a court from holding a directorship;
- over 70 years of age.

f This document sets out the company's name, the address of the company's registered office and the object of the company.

g Private companies limited by shares, private companies limited by guarantee, private unlimited companies, public limited companies.

h You cannot:

- register the same name as another company;
- use certain words;
- use names likely to cause offence.

i Every company must ~~have formally appointed company officers~~ at all times.

A private company must have at least:

- one director;
- one secretary – formal qualifications are not required. A company's sole director cannot also be the company secretary.

A public company must have at least:

- two directors;
- one secretary – formally qualified.

In most countries companies with **limited liability**, or **corporations**, are formed by **registration** at a public office or court designated by law. Each country has its own regulations for registration.

44 Articles of Association

The Articles of Association govern the running of a company and set out the rights and obligations of members and directors. Below are the main sections of the Articles of Association. The details below describe the terms and conditions in each section. Match each section to its description.

1 Share Capital g
2 Lien ______
3 Calls ______
4 Pre-emption ______
5 Transmission of Shares ______
6 Notice of Meetings ______
7 Proceedings at General Meetings ______
8 Directors ______
9 Notices ______
10 Indemnity ______
11 Winding up ______

---

a This allows the directors of the company to sell a shareholder's shares in the company to repay any debt owed by the shareholder to the company.

b This provides that any shareholder who wishes to sell his shares has to first offer them to the other shareholders at the same price as he wishes to sell to a third party.

c This provides that the directors of the company shall not be personally liable in any civil or criminal proceedings as long as they have carried out their duties lawfully.

- **d** This deals with advance information that is to be given to each member about meetings and provides that each member is allowed to appoint a proxy to attend in his place at meetings.
- **e** This requires all directors to be informed about meetings, whether they are in the country or abroad.
- **f** This allows the company to recover its costs of recovery from a late paying shareholder.
- **g** This sets out the share capital of the company.
- **h** This allows the assets of the company to be distributed if the company goes into liquidation.
- **i** This states the number of members who must be present.
- **j** This provides that when a shareholder dies he is deemed to give notice to sell his shares (which allows the other shareholders to buy them for a fair price).
- **k** This regulates the maximum number and their conduct.

Shareholder is a noun + noun combination. It is written as one word. **Share capital** is also a noun + noun combination, but it is written as two words. There are no fixed rules for writing noun + noun combinations. Typically they start as separate words, but some of them become so closely associated that they merge into one word.

45 The duties of the directors

The directors of a company are responsible for its governance. Their duties are clearly set out and, if they do not carry them out, not only may they be held liable under the law, but they may also be banned from acting as director of any company for a certain period of time.

Read through the duties and then answer the questions.

Except with the prior sanction of the holders of more than 50 per cent of the issued share capital of the Company from time to time the Directors shall procure that the Company shall not:

1 sell, transfer or otherwise dispose of the whole of its undertaking, property or (save in the ordinary course of trading) assets or a part thereof being substantial in relation to its total undertaking, property and assets;

2 issue shares, loan stock, debentures or any other form of security of the Company including for this purpose any issue of redeemable shares;

3 purchase any of its own shares;

4 incur or agree to incur any capital commitments in excess of £100,000;

5 engage or dismiss any person as a Director;

6 increase by more than 20 per cent the remuneration payable to any of its Directors, officers, employees, consultants or agents;

7 dismiss any employee;

8 purchase or sell, take or let on lease or tenancy or otherwise acquire or dispose of any real or leasehold property for any estate or interest;

9 institute any litigation save in respect of the debts owing to it in the ordinary course of business;

10 acquire or dispose or any shares, debentures, debenture stock or other securities in any other company.

Which clause states that the director shall, unless agreed by others, ensure that the company does not:

a	buy its own shares?	3
b	appoint or fire another director?	______
c	buy land?	______
d	bring a case to court except to collect money owed?	______
e	increase the pay to staff above a certain percentage?	______
f	issue equities?	______
g	spend more than a stated amount?	______
h	buy shares in another company?	______
i	sell the company or part of it?	______
j	fire an employee?	______

Notice the use of prepositions after verbs to indicate trends, for example **increase**, **rise**, **go up**, **decrease**, **fall**, **drop**, **go down**.

increase **by** *more than 20 per cent the remuneration payable* (difference)
increase **to** *£x the remuneration payable* (final level)

46 Shareholders' Agreement

The Shareholders' Agreement is intended to govern the relationship between a number of shareholders in a company. Although the Articles of Association provides some protection for minority shareholders, it is always possible to change the Articles of Association with a 75 per cent majority. The Shareholders' Agreement works as a second layer of protection, preventing the company from being run in a manner other than has been agreed.

Here are two clauses from a Shareholders' Agreement, setting out the general duties on the shareholders. Complete the texts using the words in the box.

binding	breach	conduct	consent	default	devote
efficient	obligations	perform	promote	provisions	
~~represents~~	resources	undertake	validly		

Each of the Shareholders _represents_ to the other that it has taken all necessary other actions to enable him ____________ to accept and ____________ the ____________ required under the terms of this Agreement and that performance of the ____________ of this Agreement will not result in a ____________ of or constitute a ____________ under any agreement or other contractual restriction ____________ upon him.

The Shareholders ____________ with each other that they shall not without the prior written ____________ of the other parties while a shareholder in the Company become involved in any business other than that of the Company and that they shall during such period use all reasonable endeavours to ____________ the interests of the Company and ____________ to its business such of their respective time and attention and ____________ as are reasonably required for the ____________ and profitable ____________ of the business of the Company.

47 Share capital

Link the phrase on the left to its definition on the right.

Phrases		Definitions	
1	share capital	a	If authorized by its articles, a company may transfer profits to a fund called its 'capital redemption reserve' and use it to issue these shares to the members in proportion to their existing holdings.
2	authorized capital	b	That part of the share capital that the company has decided will only be called up if the company is being wound up and for the purposes of it being wound up.
3	issued capital	c	The amount of share capital stated in the articles of association.
4	allotment of shares	d	That part of the issued capital on which the company has not requested payment.
5	nominal value	e	The process by which people become members of a company.
6	bonus shares	f	The amount of share capital the company will have.
7	paid-up capital	g	The issued capital which has been fully or partly paid-up by the shareholders.
8	uncalled capital	h	The excess paid above a share's nominal value.
9	reserve capital	i	A company's authorized share capital is divided into shares of a symbolic value. The real value of the shares may change over time, reflecting what the company is worth, but their symbolic value remains the same.
10	share premium	j	The value of the shares issued to shareholders, i.e. the nominal value of the shares rather than their actual worth.

When a company is **formed**, the person or people forming it decide whether its members' **liability** will be limited by **shares**. The members must agree to take some, or all, of the shares when the company is **registered**. The articles of association (see Test 44) must show the names of the people who have agreed to own shares and the number of shares each will own. These people are called the **subscribers**.

48 The Annual General Meeting (AGM)

Here is a sample form of the notice of invitation to an AGM. Complete the missing information using the words/phrases in the box.

accounts	auditors	Board	dividend	held	~~hereby~~	member
poll	proxy	purpose	reappoint	registered	report	vote

BACO LIMITED

NOTICE IS HEREBY **GIVEN** that the fifth Annual General Meeting of the Company will be ____________ at BACO House on 15th January 2001 at 2.00 pm for the ____________ of carrying on the business as is stated below:

1 To receive the ____________ of the Company and the Directors' ____________ for the year ended 30th September 2000.

2 To approve the declaration of a final ____________ of £87.32.

3 To reappoint Grabbit and Wrun as ____________ of the Company.

4 To ____________ John Bailey and Leslie Cohen as Directors of the Company.

Dated 19th October 2000

By Order of the ____________
Jeremy Saunders
Secretary

____________ Office:
BACO House
Tewkesbury Road
Oldhampton
W56 7YU

Note: A member who is entitled to attend and ____________ at this meeting is entitled to appoint a ____________ to attend and, on a ____________ , vote instead of him. A proxy need not also be a ____________ of the Company.

The Annual General Meeting is held once a year and all shareholders are invited to attend. In advance of the meeting, an invitation must be sent out.

49 Bankruptcy

Below are some key terms from the area of bankruptcy and insolvency. Match each word to its definition.

Terms

1 administration order ___j___

2 bankrupt ______

3 composition ______

4 compulsory liquidation ______

5 disqualification of directors ______

6 fraudulent trading ______

7 going concern ______

8 insolvent ______

9 liquidator ______

10 official receiver (OR) ______

11 petition ______

12 secured creditor ______

13 undischarged bankrupt ______

14 winding-up ______

Definitions

a A director found to have conducted the affairs of an insolvent company in an 'unfit' manner may be disqualified from holding any management position in a company for between 2 and 15 years.

b A written application to the court for relief or remedy.

c Someone against whom a bankruptcy order has been made.

d The procedure whereby the assets of a company (or partnership) are gathered in and realized, the liabilities met and the surplus, if any, distributed to members.

e The basis on which insolvency practitioners prefer to sell a business. Effectively it means the business continues, jobs are saved, and a higher price is obtained.

f An agreement between a debtor and his creditors whereby the creditors agree with the debtor between themselves to accept from the debtor payment of less than the amounts due to them in full satisfaction of their claim.

g The person appointed to deal with the assets and liabilities of the company or partnership once the resolution to wind up has been passed or a compulsory winding-up order has been made.

h Someone against whom a bankruptcy order has been made and who has not been discharged from bankruptcy.

i The placing of a company into liquidation as a result of an application to the court, usually by a creditor.

j A court order placing a company that is, or is likely to become, insolvent under the control of an administrator.

k Where a company has carried on business with intent to defraud creditors, or for any fraudulent purpose.

l The state of not being able to pay one's debts as they fall due or having an excess of liabilities over assets.

m The civil servant employed to head the regional offices whose responsibilities cover bankruptcies and compulsory liquidations.

n The first to be paid from the secured assets.

Bankruptcy law provides for the development of a supervised plan that allows a **debtor**, who is unable to pay his **creditors**, to resolve his debts through the division of his **assets** among his creditors. This allows the interests of all creditors to be treated with some measure of equality. Certain bankruptcy proceedings allow a debtor to stay in business and help him pay his debts. An additional purpose of bankruptcy law is to allow certain debtors to be released from their financial obligations after their assets are distributed, even if their debts have not been paid in full.

50 International Law and International Trade

There are very many organizations which play a role in regulating international trade. Below are the abbreviations of some of them. How many can you recognize?

APEC	ILO
ASEAN	IMF
BIS	ISO
CAP	ITU
Caricom	LAFTA
Comecon	NAFTA
EBRD	OAS
ECB	OAU/AEC
EEC	OECD
EFTA	OEEC
EU	OPEC
Euratom	UN
GATT	UNCTAD
IADB	WCO
IBRD	WTO

51 Introduction to Alternative Dispute Resolution (ADR)

Alternative Dispute Resolution (ADR) refers to a variety of procedures for the resolution of disputes. Common to all ADR procedures is the word alternative. Each ADR procedure is an alternative to court adjudication.

Read the following statements about ADR and then answer the true/false questions below.

- ADR is a voluntary process.
- The various types of ADR are all confidential.
- The mediator is a trained, neutral third party.
- The objective of ADR is to define the interests involved and reach solutions which are practical and beneficial to all parties.
- ADR is less expensive than litigation.
- ADR is faster than litigation.
- ADR allows the parties to keep the proceedings private.
- All the parties involved in the dispute should attend the ADR proceedings.
- Ideally ADR should be conducted in a neutral site.

Are the following statements true or false?

1. Anyone can act as a mediator. *True*
2. The proceedings in ADR are slower than in the traditional courts. ______
3. For ADR to work, all parties must agree to mediation. ______
4. ADR is usually cheaper than bringing a case to court. ______
5. The legal representatives of the parties can bring the case before an ADR tribunal. ______
6. ADR proceedings are held in a public court. ______
7. ADR aims to find a solution to a dispute that all parties can benefit from. ______

Alternative Dispute Resolution involves methods of resolving disputes other than through litigation. The methods are in addition to litigation and are by no means intended to replace litigation. Even the strongest proponents of ADR agree that certain matters must be resolved through the courts.

52 Arbitration

Arbitration is a procedure for the resolution of disputes on a private basis through the appointment of an arbitrator, an independent, neutral third person who hears and considers the merits of the dispute and renders a final and binding decision called an award.

A Complete the following text about arbitration with words from the box.

adjudication arbitration arbitrator decision-maker dispute documentation duration expensive expert forum hearing ~~litigation~~ needs submissions

The process is similar to the _litigation_ process as it involves ____________. However, the parties choose their ____________ and the manner in which the ____________ will proceed. For example, if the ____________ is fairly straightforward and does not involve any factual questions, the parties may agree to waive a formal ____________ and provide the arbitrator with written ____________ and ____________ only, called a documents only arbitration. However, in other cases the parties may wish a full hearing. Therefore, the parties create their own adjudicatory ____________ which is tailor-made to the particular ____________ of the parties and the nature of the dispute.

The advantages of arbitration over court adjudication can include the following:

- Expertise of the ____________: The parties can choose an arbitrator who has ____________ knowledge of the law, business or trade in which the dispute has arisen.
- Low cost: Arbitration is not ____________ if the process is kept simple.
- Speed: Arbitration can be arranged within days, weeks or months.
- ____________: Arbitration does not take as long as litigation.

B We have seen the noun 'arbitration' and the verb 'arbitrate'. Now complete the missing words in the table.

Noun	Verb
submission	*submit*
litigation	
	adjudicate
documentation	
decision	
	arrange

53 Mediation

Complete the crossword based on key words associated with mediation.

Across

5 Person who helps things happen.

7 One advantage of mediation – the price.

8 Speak while another is speaking.

10 Bargaining in order to find agreement. (noun)

13 Willingness to provide information.

15 Result of agreement between the parties.

17 Mediation is an effective _________ to resolve disputes.

18 Fast. (noun)

19 Having special ability. (adj)

Down

1 The mediator aims to find common _________ .

2 Both sides often have to _________ to reach agreement.

3 The mediator aims to bring the parties to a _________ of the dispute.

4 Both sides must accept these. (2 words)

6 An arbitrator is an _________ third party, who is not biased.

9 Willing.

11 Disagreement.

12 First the mediator learns the _________ of the parties.

14 Outcomes.

16 The mediator must _________ to the details of the dispute.

The most popular form of ADR is mediation. Mediation is a process of dispute resolution focused on effective communication and negotiation skills.

54 International commercial arbitration

International commercial arbitration is based on the same principles as domestic arbitration except it takes place between companies. The International Court of Arbitration of the International Chamber of Commerce is the arbitration body attached to the ICC. The function of the court is to provide for the settlement by arbitration of business disputes of an international character in accordance with the ICC's arbitration rules.

Below is a summary of the work and workings of the court. Match the descriptions to the headings.

Headings

1 Function c

2 Composition of the Court ______

3 Plenary Sessions of the Court ______

4 Appointment ______

5 Committees ______

6 Confidentiality ______

7 Number of Arbitrators ______

8 Request for Arbitration ______

9 Answer to the Request ______

Descriptions

a The work of the Court is of a confidential nature which must be respected by everyone who participates in that work in whatever capacity. The Court lays down the rules regarding the persons who can attend the meetings of the Court and its Committees and who are entitled to have access to the materials submitted to the Court and its Secretariat.

b Within 30 days from the receipt of the Request from the Secretariat, the Respondent shall file an Answer.

c The Court does not itself settle disputes. It has the function of ensuring the application of the Rules of Arbitration.

d The Court may set up one or more Committees and establish the functions and organization of such Committees.

e The Court shall consist of a Chairman, Vice-Chairmen, and members and alternate members (collectively designated as members). In its work it is assisted by its Secretariat (Secretariat of the Court).

f The dispute shall be decided by a sole Arbitrator or by three Arbitrators.

g The Plenary Sessions of the Court are presided over by the Chairman, or, in his absence, by one of the Vice-Chairmen designated by him.

h A party wishing to have recourse to arbitration under these Rules shall submit its Request for Arbitration to the Secretariat, which shall notify the Claimant and Respondent of the receipt of the Request and the date of such receipt.

i The Chairman is elected by the ICC Council upon recommendation of the Executive Board of the ICC.

55 Introduction to international law

International Law (or Public International Law) consists of rules and principles which govern the relations and dealings of nations with each other. It concerns itself only with questions of rights between several nations or nations and the citizens or subjects of other nations. In contrast, Private International Law deals with controversies between private persons, natural or juridical, arising out of situations having significant relationship to more than one nation. In recent years the line between public and private international law has become increasingly uncertain, because issues of private international law may also involve issues of public international law, and *vice versa*.

Look at the following legal areas and classify them into Public International Law or Private International Law.

~~adoption~~ arms control asylum contractual relations divorce ~~environmental issues~~ human rights immigration international crime maritime law piracy war crimes

Public International Law	Private International Law
environmental issues	*adoption*

Immigration is the movement of people to a new country; **emigration** is the movement of people from a country.

56 Public International Law

Below is a short text on the sources of Public International Law. Read through the text and then find the definitions of the key words.

Public International Law derives its authority from three main sources.

1 Treaties and international conventions are written agreements concluded by two or more sovereign nations or by a nation and an international organization, such as the European Union. The power to enter into treaty relations is an essential attribute of sovereignty. There is a cardinal law of international law that treaties validly concluded must not be broken by the signatories. This source is also known as conventional international law.

2 International agreements or conventions create law for the parties of the agreement. They may also lead to the creation of customary international law when they are intended for adherence generally and are in fact widely accepted. Treaties and conventions were, at first, restricted in their effects to those countries that ratified them. They are particular, not general, international law; yet regulations and procedures contained in treaties and conventions have often developed into general customary usage, that is, have come to be considered binding even on those states that did not sign and ratify them. Some customs may become part of international law because of general acceptance by most nations, even if not embodied in a written treaty instrument.

3 General principles common to systems of national law fall into the same category and are, in fact, often difficult to distinguish from customs as a source of international law.

Word		Definition	
1	convention	a	the customary method of performing or carrying out an activity that is followed by a particular group of people
2	sovereign	b	to give formal approval to something in order that it can become law
3	conclude	c	self-governing and not ruled by another state
4	binding	d	rule
5	treaty	e	legally required
6	usage	f	the action of following a rule or keeping to an agreement
7	custom	g	legally binding agreement between states sponsored by an international organization
8	regulation	h	legally binding agreement between two or more states
9	adherence	i	a formal legal document
10	ratify	j	a long established tradition or usage that becomes customary law if it is (a) consistently and regularly observed and (b) recognized by those states observing it as a practice that they must follow
11	instrument	k	to make a formal agreement complete and fixed, especially after long discussions or arrangements

57 The United Nations (UN)

The UN, an intergovernmental organization established in 1945 as the successor to the League of Nations, is concerned with the maintenance of international peace and security. Its headquarters are in New York City. On December 10, 1948, the Declaration of Human Rights was issued, defining the civil, political, economic, social and cultural rights of human beings. Below are extracts from the first 10 articles (there are 30 in all). Complete the text by choosing the correct word from the box.

charge	detention	discrimination	exile	~~free~~	freedoms	law
liberty	punishment	race	remedy	rights	slavery	tribunal

Article 1. All human beings are born ___free___ and equal in dignity and rights.
Article 2. Everyone is entitled to all the rights and __________ set forth in this Declaration, without distinction of any kind, such as __________ , colour, sex, language, religion, political or other opinion, national or social origin, property, birth or other status.
Article 3. Everyone has the right to life, __________ and security of person.
Article 4. No one shall be held in __________ or servitude; slavery and the slave trade shall be prohibited in all their forms.
Article 5. No one shall be subjected to torture or to cruel, inhuman or degrading treatment or __________ .
Article 6. Everyone has the right to recognition everywhere as a person before the __________ .
Article 7. All are equal before the law and are entitled without any __________ to equal protection of the law.
Article 8. Everyone has the right to an effective __________ by the competent national tribunals for acts violating the fundamental rights granted him by the constitution or by law.
Article 9. No one shall be subjected to arbitrary arrest, __________ or __________ .
Article 10. Everyone is entitled in full equality to a fair and public hearing by an independent and impartial __________ , in the determination of his __________ and obligations and of any criminal __________ against him.

58 The International Court of Justice

The International Court of Justice is the principal judicial body of the United Nations. Its seat is in The Hague (Netherlands). It began work in 1946, when it replaced the Permanent Court of International Justice which had functioned in The Hague since 1922.

Below is some information about the court and its activities. Match the information to the following headings. You will need to use some of the headings more than once.

- Functions of the Court
- Composition
- The Parties in Cases between States
- Jurisdiction in Cases between States
- Procedure in Cases between States
- Sources of Applicable Law
- Advisory Opinions

International Court of Justice	Headings
One of the roles of the Court is to settle in accordance with international law the legal disputes submitted to it by States.	*Functions of the Court*
The Court decides in accordance with international treaties and conventions in force, international custom, the general principles of law and, as subsidiary means, judicial decisions and the teachings of the most highly qualified publicists.	
The Members of the Court do not represent their governments but are independent magistrates.	
The advisory procedure of the Court is open solely to international organizations.	
The Court is competent to entertain a dispute only if the States concerned have accepted its jurisdiction.	
The other role is to give advisory opinions on legal questions referred to it by duly authorized international organs and agencies.	
Only States may apply to and appear before the Court.	
The Court is composed of 15 judges elected to nine-year terms of office by the United Nations General Assembly and Security Council.	
After the oral proceedings, the Court deliberates in camera and then delivers its judgement at a public sitting.	
If one of the States involved fails to comply with it, the other party may have recourse to the Security Council of the United Nations.	
The Court may not include more than one judge of any nationality.	
The judgement is final and without appeal.	

59 The International Criminal Court

Rome Statute of the International Criminal Court

'In the prospect of an international criminal court lies the promise of universal justice. That is the simple and soaring hope of this vision. We are close to its realization. We will do our part to see it through till the end. We ask you . . . to do yours in our struggle to ensure that no ruler, no State, no junta and no army anywhere can abuse human rights with impunity. Only then will the innocents of distant wars and conflicts know that they, too, may sleep under the cover of justice; that they, too, have rights, and that those who violate those rights will be punished.'

Kofi Annan, United Nations Secretary-General

Read the following objectives of the International Criminal Court and then answer the questions on the next page.

1 To achieve justice for all

2 To end impunity for abuse of human rights

3 To help end conflicts

4 To remedy the deficiencies of ad hoc tribunals

5 To take over when national criminal justice institutions are unwilling or unable to act

6 To deter future war criminals

Which objective means/suggests the following?

a Those who commit murder are often not punished. 2

b The International Criminal Court aims to discourage war criminals through the possibility of trial. ______

c Courts set up specifically to try war criminals do not deliver justice. ______

d Not everyone receives a fair trial. ______

e Local courts may not always be able to deliver justice. ______

f The International Criminal Court will try to stop wars. ______

Notice the difference in meaning between **take over** and **overtake**.

Take over: obtain or assume control of something, or gain control of something from somebody else

Overtake: to catch up with and pass a person or vehicle travelling in the same direction

60 The United Nations International Commission on Trade Law

The United Nations International Commission on Trade Law (UNCITRAL) is the core legal body of the United Nations system in the field of international trade law. As we move towards 'one world of commerce' we will increasingly need 'one commercial law'.

First read through the key areas with which UNCITRAL is involved. Then find the words/phrases in this text with the closest meanings to the definitions in the table.

UNCITRAL

- Worldwide acceptable conventions, model laws and rules
- Legal and legislative guides and recommendations of great practical value
- Updated information on case law and enactments of uniform commercial law
- Technical assistance in law reform projects
- Regional and national seminars on uniform commercial law
- Sale of goods, arbitration, electronic commerce, procurement, negotiable instruments, project finance, insolvency, countertrade, construction contracts, guarantees, receivables financing, letters of credit, maritime transport

Definitions	Words/phrases in the text
bankruptcy	*insolvency*
law established on the basis of previous verdicts, rather than law established by legislation	
accounts that are due to be paid	
the movement of goods by sea	
a letter from a bank, usually for presentation to another branch or bank, authorizing it to issue credit or money to the person named	
measures with legal force	
support	
being the same as another	
a procedure for the resolution of disputes	
a system of international trade in which countries exchange goods or services, rather than paying for imports with currency	
suggestions	
agreements	
building agreements	
process to buy and sell through the Internet	
the latest or most modern	
purchase	

Answers

Test 1

1 tribunal
2 the judiciary
3 legislation
4 rule
5 legal action
6 court
7 law enforcement agency
8 judge
9 legal system
10 authority
11 lawyers
12 govern

Test 2

Why do we have laws and **legal systems**? At one level, laws can be seen as a type of **rule** which is meant to **govern** behaviour between people. We can find these rules in nearly all social organizations, such as families and sports clubs.

Law, the body of official rules and regulations, generally found in constitutions and **legislation**, is used to govern a society and to control the behaviour of its members. In modern societies, a body with **authority**, such as a **court** or the legislature, makes the law; and a **law enforcement agency**, such as the police, makes sure it is observed.

In addition to enforcement, a body of expert **lawyers** is needed to apply the law. This is the role of **the judiciary**, the body of **judges** in a particular country. Of course, legal systems vary between countries, as well as the basis for bringing a case before a court or **tribunal**. One thing, however, seems to be true all over the world – starting a **legal action** is both expensive and time-consuming.

Test 3

A

Roman law, which evolved in the 8th century BC, was still largely a blend of custom and interpretation by magistrates of the will of the gods.

Common law evolved from the tribal and local laws in England. It began with common customs, but over time it involved the courts in law-making that was responsive to changes in society. In this way the Anglo-Norman rulers created a system of centralized courts that operated under a single set of laws that replaced the rules laid down by earlier societies.

The Ten Commandments formed the basis of all Israelite legislation. They can also be found in the laws of other ancient peoples.

Napoleonic Code refers to the entire body of French law, contained in five codes dealing with civil, commercial, and criminal law.

B

1 True.
2 False. This is the basis of Roman law.
3 False. This is the basis of common law.
4 True.

Test 4

A

Criminal	**Civil**
to charge someone with something	plaintiff
crime	compensation
police	contract
prosecution	damages
the accused	family law
the defendant	intellectual property
theft	private individual
to bring a case	the defendant
to fine	to bring a case
	to bring an action

B

Criminal Law vs Civil Law

One category is the criminal law – the law dealing with **crime**. A case is called a **prosecution**. The case is instituted by the prosecutor, who takes over the case from the **police** who have already decided **to charge** the defendant (or **accused**) with specified crimes. The civil law is much more wide-ranging. The civil law includes the law of **contract** and **family law** (or **intellectual property**). In a civil case, the **plaintiff**, normally a **private individual** or company, **brings an action** to win **compensation**. If the case is proven (on the balance of probabilities, meaning that one is more sure than not), the defendant normally pays the plaintiff **damages** (money).

Test 5

1 County Court
2 Court of Appeal, Criminal Division
3 House of Lords
4 Crown Court
5 Magistrates Court
6 High Court
7 Court of Justice of the European Communities
8 Court of Appeal, Civil Division

Test 6

A

C J U G U I O P P P P O M T

H N O E U Z V U P L F T N **P**

G L O **M** C V U Q **J** B L **R** E **R**

N A S **A** D R T **J U D G E** N **O**

C H I **G** E T Y T **R** B O **C** P **S**

J U D I C I A R Y A S **O** Y **E**

P L E **S** F L E S F T A **R** Y **C**

M O L **T** A X R T E V B **D** A **U**

A **B A R R I S T E R** G **E** L **T**

T **E** R **A** A T H I L K G **R** G **O**

A **N** O **T** H E T M P L O X C **R**

A **C L E R K** M L O I R T U K

C **H** Y H A N B C T P O L T Z

X P L E **P R E S I D E N T** A

B

The **judiciary** are perhaps the most prominent amongst those involved in running the court. The largest group of **judges** are **magistrates**, ordinary citizens who are not legal professionals but are appointed to ensure that the local community is involved in the running of the legal system. They sit as a group of three (as a '**bench**'). Magistrates sit with a legally qualified **clerk**, who can advise on points of law. A case is presented by the **prosecutor**, who takes over the case from the police who have already charged the defendant (or accused) with specified crimes.

In the upper courts, the judges are almost all former **barristers**. But many cases are also heard by **recorders** – part-time barristers from private practice. The Crown Court **jury** consists of 12 persons, aged 18 to 70.

Test 7

Solicitors

advocacy in the lower courts
advising clients on general legal issues
advising on tax matters
commercial work
conveyancing of houses
dealing with commercial transactions
making wills
preparing cases
share and other property dealings

Barristers

advocacy in all courts
advising clients on specialist legal issues
advising on litigation
drafting of documents in connection with litigation

Test 8

5 6 3 7 2 4 1

Test 9

A

1 of
2 for
3 to
4 for
5 to
6 against
7 of
8 for

B

1 accused, of, was guilty of, sentence, to, fined, for
2 brought a case against, claimed damages for, was liable for, was entitled to

Test 10

1	judiciary	10	barrister
2	judge	11	solicitor
3	common law	12	magistrate
4	Roman law	13	defendant
5	criminal law	14	legislation
6	prosecutor	15	authority
7	plaintiff	16	pupillage
8	damages	17	tenancy
9	jury	18	House of Lords

Test 11

A

1	obligation	8	signed
2	agreement	9	property
3	consideration	10	breach
4	capacity	11	damages
5	fraud	12	performance
6	illegal	13	terms
7	oral		

Test 12

1	f	4	a	7	i
2	b	5	g	8	e
3	d	6	c	9	h

Test 13

1	f	6	g	11	h
2	d	7	m	12	j
3	k	8	e	13	c
4	i	9	l		
5	a	10	b		

Test 14

1	e	5	a	9	g
2	c	6	j	10	i
3	h	7	d		
4	f	8	b		

Test 15

Reminder 1	2	6
Reminder 2	4	1
Reminder 3	7	5
Final demand	3	

Test 16

a	2	f	9
b	3	g	1
c	7	h	6
d	10	i	5
e	8	j	4

Test 17

1	True	5	False
2	False	6	False
3	True	7	True
4	True	8	False

Test 18

1	terms	9	debit
2	conditions	10	account
3	repayment	11	instalment
4	capital	12	bank base rate
5	loan	13	increase
6	interest	14	decrease
7	payment	15	repay
8	arrears	16	penalty

Test 19

1	j	7	g
2	h	8	d
3	c	9	b
4	a	10	k
5	f	11	e
6	i		

Test 20

DUTIES

2.1 Subject as hereinafter **provided** and except at such times as the Consultant may be incapacitated by **illness** or accident, the Consultant shall devote such of his time, **attention** and skill as may be necessary for the proper discharge of his duties, save that nothing in this Agreement shall require the Consultant to devote to his **obligations** under this Agreement more than 60 hours **monthly**.

2.2 The Consultant shall keep the Board of Directors of the Company ('the Board') **informed** of progress on projects in which the Consultant is engaged and shall produce **written** reports on the same from time to time when so **requested** by the Board. While the Consultant's method of work is his own, he shall comply with the **reasonable** requests of the Board and shall work and co-operate with any **servant** or agent or other consultant of the Company.

2.3 The Consultant will not during his **engagement** [and for a period of twelve months thereafter] undertake any **additional** activities or accept other engagements which would **interfere** with or preclude the **performance** of his duties under this Agreement or which lead to or might lead to any conflict of **interest** between the Consultant and the best interests of the Company.

Test 21

1 position
2 duties and responsibilities
3 date of commencement
4 terms and conditions
5 probationary service
6 commencing salary
7 sickness pay
8 holiday entitlement
9 notice
10 pension
11 grievance

Test 22

Reason for the warning		
Poor work	6	d
Poor attitude	4	e
Delay	2	f
Behaviour	3	a
Punctuality	1	b
Housekeeping	5	c

Test 23

Possible answer:
6 3 5 10 9 1 8 7 2 4

Test 24

1 k	5 b	9 f
2 e	6 j	10 i
3 g	7 c	11 d
4 h	8 a	

Test 25

Across	**Down**
1 blue collar	2 entitlement
3 part time	4 maternity
6 grade	5 leave
8 supervisor	7 duties
11 notice	8 manpower
12 shift	10 vacation
13 day off	
14 subordinate	

Test 26

1 safety	9 injured
2 health	10 disabled
3 illnesses	11 monetary
4 injuries	12 dependants
5 deaths	13 workers
6 regulations	14 protection
7 dangers	15 recover
8 unsafe	16 liability

Test 27

1 e	5 j	9 c
2 f	6 i	10 g
3 h	7 a	11 l
4 k	8 d	12 b

Test 28

See page 92

Test 29

1 investigation by police
2 apprehension of suspect
3 charge of suspect
4 release on bail
5 interrogation of witnesses
6 appearance in court
7 conviction of accused
8 acquittal of accused
9 sentence by judge
10 appeal against judgement

Test 28

V or NV	Name of crime	Definition of crime
V	assault	attempt to use illegal force on another person
NV	drug dealing	possession of and/or trading in illegal substances
NV	money laundering	attempt to transform illegally acquired money into apparently legitimate money
V	battery	the actual use of illegal force on another person
V	homicide	a generic term for the killing of another person
V	manslaughter	the unlawful killing of a person without malicious intent and therefore without premeditation
NV	fraud	any instance in which one party deceives or takes unfair advantage of another
V	murder	the unlawful killing of a person with intent
V	armed robbery	the unlawful taking of another's property using a dangerous weapon
V	sexual assault	attempt to use illegal force on another person in the absence of consent to sexual relations
NV	burglary	the crime of breaking into a private home with the intention of committing a felony
NV	theft	taking the property of another without right or permission
NV	parking	leaving one's vehicle in an area or for a duration in contravention of the law
NV	speeding	driving a vehicle in excess of the permitted limit

Test 30

a 7
b 11
c 15
d 3
e 1
f 5
g 8
h 14
i 10
j 2
k 16
l 4
m 6
n 12
o 9
p 13

Test 31

1 h
2 n
3 c
4 e
5 j
6 m
7 a
8 i
9 g
10 k
11 d
12 l
13 b
14 f

Test 32

1 False
2 True
3 True
4 True
5 False
6 True
7 True
8 False

Test 33

The police interrogate suspects and witnesses.
The police carry out arrests, searches, and seizures.
The magistrate sometimes conducts the investigation in cases of serious criminal offences.
The prosecutor conducts the case in court on behalf of the police.
The suspect has the right to remain silent.
The suspect is innocent until proved guilty.
The defence counsel assists the suspect in gathering exonerating evidence.
The defence counsel protects the suspect from violations of his rights at the hands of law-enforcement personnel.
The judge presides over the court.
The judge decides on the sentence to be imposed.
The jury decides whether the accused is guilty or not.

Test 34

A

1 c	4 a	7 b
2 h	5 g	8 f
3 e	6 d	

B

Appellate procedure consists of the rules and practices by which a **court of appeal** reviews trial court judgements. The procedure focuses on several main themes:

- what judgements are **appealable**,
- how an **appeal** is to be brought before the court,
- what will be required for a reversal of the lower court,
- what procedures the parties must follow

Often an **appeal bond** will be put up to pay the other side's costs in case the appeal fails.
Normally **leave to appeal** will be requested by the **appellant**, who is seeking a review of the decision of a subordinate court or person. The other party, the **appellee**, is usually, but not always, the winner in the lower court.

Test 35

Areas	**Branches**
Product Liability	Accident and Injury Compensation and Prevention
Civil Rights	Constitutional Law, Individual Rights
Pensions	Employment Law
Joint Ventures	Enterprise Law
Divorce	Family Law
Unfair Competition	Intellectual Property
Foreign Relations Law	International, Transnational, Comparative Law
Landlord–Tenant	Law relating to Commercial Transactions
Agriculture	Law relating to Particular Activities/ Business Sectors
Environmental Law	Property, Natural Resources, the Environment
Property Tax	Taxation

Test 36

1. Banking
2. Bankruptcy
3. Commercial Law
4. Consumer Credit
5. Contracts
6. Debtor and Creditor
7. Landlord and Tenant
8. Mortgages
9. Negotiable Instruments
10. Real Estate Transactions
11. Sales
12. Secured Transactions

bankruptcy
mortgage

Test 37

See page 94

Test 38

A

atomic energy
clean water
clean air
endangered species
energy sources
natural resources
navigable waters
noise pollution
ocean dumping
oil pollution
pesticide control
tropical forests
waste disposal

B

1. tropical forests
2. clean water
3. pesticide control
4. ocean dumping
5. noise pollution
6. endangered species

Test 39

Across	**Down**
1 novel	2 original
3 false	4 approval
7 limited	5 infringement
10 inventor	6 discover
12 exclusive	8 register
15 author	9 trademark
16 copyright	11 writings
17 authorized	13 patent
	14 protect

Test 37

Terms (1)	Terms (2)	Definitions (1)	Definitions (2)
attorney	client	a person authorized to act on another's behalf as a lawyer	a person who buys the services of another, in this case legal services
executor	heir	a person specifically appointed by a testator to administer the will ensuring that final wishes are respected (i.e. that the will is properly 'executed')	a person entitled to receive under the terms of a will
trustee	beneficiary	a natural or legal person to whom property is committed to be administered for the benefit of a beneficiary (as a person or charitable organization)	a person or entity named or otherwise entitled to receive the principal or income or both from a trust
master	servant	an individual or entity (as a corporation) having control or authority over another	a person who serves others
guardian	ward	an individual who, by legal appointment or by the effect of a written law, is given custody of both the property and the person of one who is unable to manage his own affairs, such as a child or mentally-disabled person	a person who by reason of incapacity is under the control of another
corporate director	stockholder	an officer appointed by the shareholders to represent their interests	an owner of corporate stock
employer	employee	one that hires others to perform a service or engage in an activity in exchange for compensation	a person hired by another to perform a service especially for wages or salary and who is under the other's control

Test 40

1 Adoption
2 Child Custody
3 Children's Rights
4 Divorce
5 Estate Planning
6 Estates and Trusts
7 Insurance
8 Marriage

Test 41

1 Compensatory damages and punitive damages.
The former are intended to compensate the injured party for his loss or injury; the latter are awarded to punish a wrongdoer.
2 the individual suffering the loss; the individual causing the loss via negligence or unlawful conduct; a particular party who has been allocated the burden by the legislature, such as employers under Workmen's Compensation statutes.
3 the manufacturer of component parts; an assembling manufacturer; the wholesaler; the retail store owner
4 sue for an injunction to prevent the continuation of the tortious conduct; sue for monetary damages
5 injured or disabled employees, and dependants of injured or disabled employees

Test 42

A company is a **legal** entity, allowed by **legislation**, which permits a group of people, as **shareholders**, to create an organization, which can then focus on pursuing set **objectives**. It is empowered with legal rights which are usually only reserved for individuals, such as the right to **sue** and be sued, own **property**, hire **employees** or loan and **borrow** money. The primary advantage of a company structure is that it provides the shareholders with a right to participate in the **dividends**, a proportionate distribution of profits made in the form of a money payment to shareholders, without any personal **liability**.

There are various forms of legal business entities ranging from the **sole trader**, who alone bears the risk and responsibility of running a business, taking the profits, but as such not forming any association in law and thus not regulated by special rules of law, to the **registered** company with **limited** liability and to multinational **corporations**.

In a **partnership**, members 'associate,' forming collectively an association in which they all participate in management and sharing **profits**, bearing the liability for the firm's **debts** and being sued jointly and severally in relation to the firm's contracts or tortious acts.

Limited-liability companies, or corporations, unlike partnerships, are formed not simply by **agreements** entered into between their first members; they must also be **registered** at a public office or **court** designated by law or otherwise obtain official acknowledgement of their existence.

Test 43

1 c	4 i	7 d
2 e	5 a	8 b
3 g	6 h	9 f

Test 44

1 g	5 j	9 e
2 a	6 d	10 c
3 f	7 i	11 h
4 b	8 k	

Test 45

a 3	f 2
b 5	g 4
c 8	h 10
d 9	i 1
e 6	j 7

Test 46

Each of the Shareholders **represents** to the other that it has taken all necessary other actions to enable him **validly** to accept and **perform** the **obligations** required under the terms of this Agreement and that performance of the **provisions** of this Agreement will not result in a **breach** of or constitute a **default** under any agreement or other contractual restriction **binding** upon him.

The Shareholders **undertake** with each other that they shall not without the prior written **consent** of the other parties while a shareholder in the Company become involved in any business other than that of the Company and that they shall during such period use all reasonable endeavours to **promote** the interests of the Company and **devote** to its business such of their respective time and attention and **resources** as are reasonably required for the **efficient** and profitable **conduct** of the business of the Company.

Test 47

1 f	5 i	9 b
2 c	6 a	10 h
3 j	7 g	
4 e	8 d	

Test 48

BACO LIMITED

NOTICE IS HEREBY GIVEN that the fifth Annual General Meeting of the Company will be **held** at BACO House on 15th January 2001 at 2.00 pm for the **purpose** of carrying on the business as is stated below:

1. To receive the **accounts** of the Company and the Directors' **report** for the year ended 30th September 2000.
2. To approve the declaration of a final **dividend** of £87.32.
3. To reappoint Grabbit and Wrun as **auditors** of the Company.

4 To **reappoint** John Bailey and Leslie Cohen as Directors of the Company.

Dated 19th October 2000

By Order of the **Board**
Jeremy Saunders
Secretary

Registered Office:
BACO House
Tewkesbury Road
Oldhampton
W56 7YU

Note: A member who is entitled to attend and **vote** at this meeting is entitled to appoint a **proxy** to attend and, on a **poll**, vote instead of him. A proxy need not also be a **member** of the Company.

Test 49

1 j	6 k	11 b
2 c	7 e	12 n
3 f	8 l	13 h
4 i	9 g	14 d
5 a	10 m	

Test 51

1 True.
However, they must be trained as a mediator.
2 False.
3 True.
4 True.
5 False.
6 False.
7 True.

Test 50

APEC	Asia Pacific Economic Co-operation
ASEAN	Association of Southeast Asian Nations
BIS	Bank for International Settlements
CAP	Common Agricultural Policy
Caricom	Caribbean Community and Common Market
Comecon	Council for Mutual Economic Assistance
EBRD	European Bank for Reconstruction and Development
ECB	European Central Bank
EEC	European Economic Community
EFTA	European Free Trade Association
EU	European Union
Euratom	European Atomic Energy Community
GATT	General Agreement on Tariffs and Trade
IADB	Inter-American Development Bank
IBRD	International Bank for Reconstruction and Development
ILO	International Labour Organization
IMF	International Monetary Fund
ISO	International Standardization Organization
ITU	International Telecommunications Union
LAFTA	Latin American Free Trade Association
NAFTA	North American Free Trade Agreement
OAS	Organization of American States
OAU/AEC	Organization of African Unity/African Economic Community
OECD	Organization for Economic Co-operation and Development
OEEC	Organization for European Economic Co-operation
OPEC	Organization of the Petroleum Exporting Countries
UN	United Nations
UNCTAD	United Nations Conference on Trade and Development
WCO	World Customs Organization
WTO	World Trade Organization

Test 52

A

The process is similar to the **litigation** process as it involves **adjudication**. However, the parties choose their **arbitrator** and the manner in which the **arbitration** will proceed. For example, if the **dispute** is fairly straightforward and does not involve any factual questions, the parties may agree to waive a formal **hearing** and provide the arbitrator with written **submissions** and **documentation** only, called a documents only arbitration. However, in other cases the parties may wish a full hearing. Therefore, the parties create their own adjudicatory **forum** which is tailor-made to the particular **needs** of the parties and the nature of the dispute.

The advantages of arbitration over court adjudication can include the following:

- Expertise of the **decision-maker**: The parties can choose an arbitrator who has **expert** knowledge of the law, business or trade in which the dispute has arisen.
- Low cost: Arbitration is not **expensive** if the process is kept simple.
- Speed: Arbitration can be arranged within days, weeks or months.
- **Duration**: Arbitration does not take as long as litigation.

B

Noun	**Verb**
submission	submit
litigation	litigate
adjudication	adjudicate
documentation	document
decision	decide
arrangement	arrange

Test 53

Across		**Down**	
5	facilitator	1	ground
7	cost	2	compromise
8	interrupt	3	discussion
10	negotiation	4	ground rules
13	openness	6	independent
15	settlement	9	voluntary
17	process	11	dispute
18	speed	12	positions
19	skilful	14	results
		16	listen

Test 54

1	c	4	i	7	f
2	e	5	d	8	h
3	g	6	a	9	b

Test 55

Public International Law

environmental issues
arms control
asylum
human rights
immigration
international crime
maritime law
piracy
war crimes

Private International Law

adoption
contractual relations
divorce

Test 56

1	g	5	h	9	f
2	c	6	a	10	b
3	k	7	j	11	i
4	e	8	d		

Test 57

Article 1. All human beings are born **free** and equal in dignity and rights.
Article 2. Everyone is entitled to all the rights and **freedoms** set forth in this Declaration, without distinction of any kind, such as **race**, colour, sex, language, religion, political or other opinion, national or social origin, property, birth or other status.

Article 3. Everyone has the right to life, **liberty** and security of person.
Article 4. No one shall be held in **slavery** or servitude; slavery and the slave trade shall be prohibited in all their forms.
Article 5. No one shall be subjected to torture or to cruel, inhuman or degrading treatment or **punishment**.
Article 6. Everyone has the right to recognition everywhere as a person before the **law**.
Article 7. All are equal before the law and are entitled without any **discrimination** to equal protection of the law.
Article 8. Everyone has the right to an effective **remedy** by the competent national tribunals for acts violating the fundamental rights granted him by the constitution or by law.
Article 9. No one shall be subjected to arbitrary arrest, **detention** or **exile**.
Article 10. Everyone is entitled in full equality to a fair and public hearing by an independent and impartial **tribunal**, in the determination of his **rights** and obligations and of any criminal **charge** against him.

Test 58

International Court of Justice	**Headings**
• One of the roles of the Court is to settle in accordance with international law the legal disputes submitted to it by States.	Functions of the Court
• The Court decides in accordance with international treaties and conventions in force, international custom, the general principles of law and, as subsidiary means, judicial decisions and the teachings of the most highly qualified publicists.	Sources of Applicable Law
• The Members of the Court do not represent their governments but are independent magistrates.	Composition
• The advisory procedure of the Court is open solely to international organizations.	Advisory Opinions
• The Court is competent to entertain a dispute only if the States concerned have accepted its jurisdiction.	Jurisdiction in Cases between States
• The other role is to give advisory opinions on legal questions referred to it by duly authorized international organs and agencies.	Functions of the Court
• Only States may apply to and appear before the Court.	The Parties in Cases between States
• The Court is composed of 15 judges elected to nine-year terms of office by the United Nations General Assembly and Security Council.	Composition
• After the oral proceedings, the Court deliberates in camera and then delivers its judgement at a public sitting.	Procedure in Cases between States
• If one of the States involved fails to comply with it, the other party may have recourse to the Security Council of the United Nations.	Procedure in Cases between States
• The Court may not include more than one judge of any nationality.	Composition
• The judgement is final and without appeal.	Procedure in Cases between States

Test 59

a 2	d 1
b 6	e 5
c 4	f 3

Test 60

Definitions	**Words/phrases in the text**
bankruptcy	insolvency
law established on the basis of previous verdicts, rather than law established by legislation	case law
accounts that are due to be paid	receivables
the movement of goods by sea	maritime transport
a letter from a bank, usually for presentation to another branch or bank, authorizing it to issue credit or money to the person named	letters of credit
measures with legal force	enactments
support	assistance
being the same as another	uniform
a procedure for the resolution of disputes	arbitration
a system of international trade in which countries exchange goods or services, rather than paying for imports with currency	countertrade
suggestions	recommendations
agreements	conventions
building agreements	construction contracts
process to buy and sell through the Internet	electronic commerce
the latest or most modern	updated
purchase	procurement

Word list

The numbers after the entries are the tests in which they appear.

Test Your way to success in English

Test Your Professional English

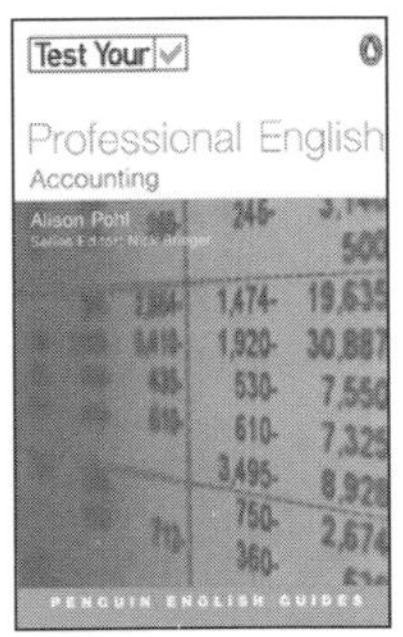

0582 45163 9

0582 45148 5

0582 45149 3

0582 45160 4

0582 45161 2

0582 46898 1

0582 46897 3

0582 45150 7

0582 45147 7

0582 45162 0

www.penguinenglish.com 

COLEG GLAN HAFREN LRC PARADE